MEMOIRS OF A SERIAL HILLER

ALAN BUTTERWORTH

Cromwell Publishers, 405 Kings Road, Chelsea, London SW10 0BB

E-mail: editorial@CromwellPublishers.co.uk

Website: www.CromwellPublishers.co.uk

Paperback ISBN 1-903930-05-7

ACKNOWLEDGEMENTS

I am deeply indebted to:

My amazing family for putting up with me, especially Sylvia for her editing.

Aunty Marjorie, for getting me started, at the age of seven.

David Prestbury, for inspiration.

Alan Rayner, for supplying the Icelandic photographs , after my camera broke.

And the main characters of this book, who have made being on the hills so much fun.

INTRODUCTION

This book is a record and a tribute to the characters, often funny, who have accompanied me at every turn and tarn on the hills over nearly four and a half decades. It is their story not mine.

This is not a how-to book, and must not be so taken. In fact, it is the very opposite.

Please excuse any lapses in geography; much of what I have written is from memory.

Although this book is intended to be humorous, please do not think for a moment that fell walking is to be taken lightly by anyone. Conditions on the fells can change dramatically within minutes. Therefore, only go on the fells if you are well prepared, which means prepared for the worst.

I personally consider that walking, especially at altitude, is the best of all medicines, not least if you are laughing much or even most of the time

1 THE START

I was born in Kendal, at the heart of the English Lakes, where they do have hills and grass and trees and other country things like farms, so maybe there was always a subconscious, but then dormant - ready to be awakened - urge to be up on higher land than that on which dusty towns reside.

Grass, as we now know it, barely had a foothold in Hulme, where I was brought up, and trees - proper ones, with gnarled trunks and uppers that caused shadows - only occupied a few posh gardens and the grounds of the odd church or school. Hills - actual hills devised by natural means - like millions of years of the earth's formation, and not caused by clearing up after a bombing raid - were never a feature of the local landscape. I didn't even get as high as our attic until I was about six because there was never a light up there, and the gloomy foreboding staircase that could be seen from my bedroom door, reached up into a very dense blackness. That blackness was, I convinced myself, a lair for a family of monsters who boiled children alive. The monsters shuffled around at night and sometimes peeped down from the gloom, beckoning with scrawny hands that had never been washed. I blame that attic for my early nightmares.

We did have bombsites in Hulme, where the Germans had laid waste to our buildings, and these clearings were soon swallowed up by nature, which saw to it that weeds grew in abundance. Sometimes the bombsites were the most botanical and colourful of what became Hulme's natural reserves. As I remembered it, the bombsites lasted forever - probably all of my childhood - and were the best places to play, where cats stalked mice and rats, as would larger cats stalk gazelles. The bombsites were our jungles and brought a certain rustic charm to the residents of Hulme, although the weeds that thrived there never quite looked the part, like the ones in proper country places.

It's amazing that years later I would be climbing up mountains with the children and grandchildren of those men who were out to remove our houses from the map. Maybe they were really only trying to kill the monsters in our attics, but had to remove the whole house just to make sure.

Being born on the twenty seventh of April 1941, I share a birthday with a certain Edward Whymper (1840-1911), an English wood engraver, who became the first person to scale the Matterhorn, so maybe my birthday does hold something special for those with an interest in the outdoor life. Anyway, I was only in Kendal to be born, and was soon in Hulme, which was being bombed, without ever seeing hills and green things. I should have stayed in Kendal, a much healthier place, in more ways than one.

Princess Road School, in Moss Side, was the scene of my early learning; a solid, heavy looking building - as were schools of yesteryear - now well gone from the scene to make way for houses. (Looking back - my old school was the most permanent of structures around. So much for appearances.) Actually there's a lot of grass about, where my school used to be, which can't be a bad thing.

Two main deficiencies came to light very quickly during my early learning years, which were never really put to right, even to this day. The first, and most crucial of these things was my inability to grasp simple mathematics especially when being pummelled into giving an immediate answer during, what was aptly called mental arithmetic. Where arithmetic was concerned, I was mental, with simple multiplication slotting into the dyslexia section of my brain. The other thing greatly lacking was the total inability of my voice to be put to any tuneful vocalised use. I could not and still can't sing a note. Now those of you who can sing even the simplest of tunes might not think that being unable to sing should be a problem. But it is, or was at my school. In class, during singing, I mimed, and had got away with it until the teacher homed in on me one day, and realised that no sound was coming from my mouth. I was ordered to the headmaster's office where I had to sing the notes of the scales, during which the headmaster looked down at his desk, shaking his head in disbelief at the grating sounds filling the room. His name was Mr Cross, and I had never seen him cross until that day. He thought that I was having him on, but not being able to prove it, sent me back to the classroom where I was never made to sing again.

The other malfunction, this time on a more social and sporting level - and a thing that bothered me less - mainly because I couldn't see the point, was my lack of skill - and interest, in ball games. My mates around where I lived, from a very early age, played football in a small square near to our houses, and as much as I tried to adapt some control over that leather-covered sphere, the thing began to have a mind of its own. In fact, as I grew, I realised that any sport or pastime that measured its success on even a simple amount of skill with a round object, was totally beyond me. In these politically correct times I would have been described as being spherically disadvantaged, and probably been in line for a local authority grant. If I went to kick a ball, it would slide off to the side somewhere, probably to an opposing player. My cricket bats became without solid matter in my hands and those horrible heavy balls that could kill would fly through the willow, sending three wooden posts and a silly little dowel in various directions. Nobody else had this knack. Later, tennis became a nightmare, and even the genteel art of badminton, which didn't even use a ball, was beyond me.

When I was about seven or eight, my Aunt Marjorie and Uncle Bill took me rambling - a new word to me - which meant, in this case, walking about round a reservoir. The reservoir we rambled around was the Combs Reservoir between Chapel-en-le-Frith and Whalley Bridge, an event that brought a whole new dimension to what I considered weekends to be used for. Green things were in abundance, like wild grasses, trees and ferns, and whilst Aunt Marjorie and Uncle Bill relaxed on the grass, I explored woods in the freedom of my own company. I climbed trees and wondered at living, hopping rabbits, rather than the bloodied, very dead variety I'd seen hanging from a butcher shop window on Alexander Road. The woods attracted me the most, reminding me of the forest background on the stage of the Hulme Hippodrome, when my family took me at Christmas to see pantomimes. It was always in the woods that the wicked witch first appeared, to the rustling of wind and the flashing of lights. Woods were wondrous and magic places where shadows prevailed and evil eyes peered from every hidden place. What a place to escape to from the dirty brick houses of Hulme, where the total confusion of mathematics did not matter and I could play, and imagine wonderful things. I was hooked.

Over the next few years other place names became part of my vocabulary; places like the Goyt Valley, Kinder Downfall, and others. Towns, such as Macclesfield, Buxton, Hayfield, Chinley and Glossop became part of my weekend life, and where people obeyed a different set of rules. People on country paths always greeted us with a kind 'good morning' and we greeted them back, well, I was made to. I had never been so polite in my life. Within a close distance to most paths there was usually an inn or cafe where people ate cakes and sipped tea without slurping, and always talked in whispered tones. I could never understand this at first. These people whispered in funny accents, a sort of contrived poshness, whilst holding tea cups delicately with their little fingers pointing to the ceiling. Men smoked pipes a lot then, especially ramblers, including Uncle Bill, and women laughed noiselessly, other than Aunty Marjorie who didn't care. I used to talk loudly in cafes using a funny accent, just to annoy people and fight off boredom, and people used to stare as if I was something brought in under their rambling boots.

Most Sunday mornings began in Stockport bus station, a place I began to have deep feelings about, where ramblers thronged, waiting for the bus of their choice, where little clouds of pipe smoke told the world that there were ramblers present. Rucksacks leaned against things like walls and handrails, and women in long tweedy skirts went to spend a penny in the bus station toilets before getting on the bus, so they wouldn't have to do it whilst rambling.

At eleven I moved to St Margaret's Central School which bordered on Whalley Range, after passing the Eleven Plus test, a fact that amazed my teachers, family, friends and mostly me. Again, my numeric dyslexia plagued me - but much worse - and here they played football. Not only did they play it but one of the teachers was the manager of Manchester Boys football team, and always liked to have at least a couple of lads from the school in the team. My inability with the ball was met with fascinated disbelief, but I had to play football with my class, it was the rules. I was always the last to be picked on anybody's team. I was good at PT, and art was my favourite classroom activity, a subject - the only subject - where I achieved good marks.

The highlight of my school years was when I went to Austria on a school trip. I was fourteen at the time. We stayed in a place near Innsbruck, part way up a steep hill, in a pension with wonderful mountain views and steep roads with hairpin bends. I was in the basement, in a room that I shared with four or five other boys. The room was inhabited by a platoon of cockroaches, which only came out at night. The cockroaches were German, wore jackboots, and knew how to march noisily, but orderly. One of the lads, the son of a vicar (or some type of church person) a quiet lad who usually kept himself to himself, shared the room with us. On the first night we were awakened from our slumbers by a deep voice bellowing: 'Tis death,' followed by a crunching sound. Then 'Tis death,' then crunch. It was the son of the vicar crunching cockroaches with a shoe. This went on for ages, during which time us lads were wetting ourselves laughing, and in the morning the floor was littered with hundreds of tiny crushed corpses, which were all swept up and carted back to the Fatherland, where they were awarded the Iron Cross posthumously.

But Austria was something else. I had never seen such mountains, or so many, and all topped with snow, everywhere you looked. I desperately wanted to climb up those mountains but we only did a couple of small walks on lower mountain paths, spending a lot of time sightseeing, to places like Innsbruck. On one of the walks we passed a man who carried a shotgun in one hand and a bloodied stag's head in another. That night we had venison for dinner, a first for all the lads, and an event that brought about varying emotions. I made a vow to go back to Austria one day, a promise that took me more than thirty years to keep.

My pals from Hulme played football whilst I went rambling, but sometimes we all went playing - if that's what you could call it - around the waterways of Manchester, the River Irwell, the Bridgewater Canal, and other lesser known mysterious and muddy locations. We knew lots of places to hide, and where we could climb up and over the grimy latticework that formed the structural parts of bridges overlooking these gloomy waters. These were dangerous times, dangling by our fingertips over black oily liquid for no other reason than it was there. These places, the hidden, dark recesses, were the homes to pigeons that flapped noisily as we disturbed their Sunday afternoon siestas. Some lads hunted pigeon eggs, for whatever reason I couldn't imagine, which was a very dangerous pastime, as these were usually over the deepest waters and in the most gloomy of recesses. River banks were thick black, greasy mud, on which we slipped, disturbing rats who ran off into the blackness, frightening the life out of me. These were our playgrounds of which I had many nightmares, and from which I retained a great fear of water, especially the black type, hidden partly by overhead steelwork.

At fifteen I joined some adults, who ran a youth club, on a trip to Windgather Rocks, in Cheshire, where they showed me how to climb rocks properly. These were nice people who whispered in cafes and were polite, other than when they saw me racing up a rock face, then they shouted at me, because I was being silly. They were quite right of course, and only thinking of my safety: but they had never climbed the greasy latticework over filthy black water, watched by rats from a riverbank. Nobody had ever said I was silly climbing those dangerous places, but then, thinking about it - and I have a lot - we were all pretty stupid then, and lucky, now, to be alive.

There were two boffin pupils at my school, who, it was rumoured, had made nitro-glycerine, a volatile explosive, and had blown up a tree in Alexander Park near to the school. These lads were held in great esteem by all others, and I befriended them in order to learn some of their dark secrets. One lunchtime I made this device in a steel tube with the ends squeezed together, with a hole in the middle where a fuse was inserted. Three of my pals watched as I dug a little hole on a bombsite near our school, then I lit the fuse and we all stood back like you do with fireworks. The blast was unbelievable, and did temporary damage to our eardrums as we ran from that place. The nearest building was a firelighter factory, which was about ten feet away from the blast, and on the other side of the wall was a woman having her lunch. Firelighters were bundles of wood held together with sawdust that was saturated with paraffin, and were used to ignite coal fires. Near to the woman was a vat of paraffin. The woman must have thought that the Germans were back, and ran screaming from that place, just in time to see us kids racing towards our school. The woman followed us and reported it all to the headmaster, who called the police, who eventually confiscated my chemistry set, and gave me the biggest telling off of my life, and said that I was lucky to not have been prosecuted. I got six of the very best of the headmaster's leather strap on my exposed bottom and gave up chemistry for good.

At fifteen I began to worry about my future, mainly because most of my teachers reckoned that I didn't have one. I had to sit a test, the Central Schools Leaving Certificate, which I amazingly just scrapped through, another fact that surprised everyone, and brought great relief to me.

But I had to get a job, and there were three no-go areas. Sums, singing and professional football, and probably chemistry now. After a brief time working on Salford Market, selling cooked meats, I managed to get an apprenticeship at Metropolitan Vickers Electrical Company in Trafford Park, where I initially spent time in a training school learning the basics of mechanical engineering skills, which went hand in hand with much discipline, then more discipline. Then out to the shop floors, where I was not immediately impressed with the biggest buildings I had ever been in. Where overhead cranes moved on tracks, carrying great steel loads over strange and massive machinery operated by faceless boiler suited men in flat caps. Smoke trailed through the air from hot coiled swarf cut out of great chunks of steel by obscure machinery.

Then there was further education, which meant going to Stretford Technical College with other apprentices, and suddenly mathematics were of the applied sort and began to make a little bit of sense because I could see a reason for it all.

At sixteen I became a Teddy boy, complete with velvet collars on drape jackets that reached my knees, drain pipe trousers, one inch wide ties and fancy waistcoats. I had sideburns down to my chin and I hung around in Granelli's cafe on Stretford Road where all proper Teddy boys were to be found. Our gang was like the Mongol Hordes and just as infamous. If you weren't a Teddy boy you went to the Court School of Dancing over Burtons on Stretford Road, with the chance that you got beat up by Teddy boys as you came out. Teddy boys jived in the aisles when Rock Around the Clock was played at a city centre picture house then thronged around the Cenotaph, clashing with police. Rock and roll was all there was, and Elvis Presley the king. Jimmy Saville, in tartan jackets and smoking cigars like rolled up carpets, played your favourite record at the Plaza, in the city centre. Little Richard sang Lucille with so much emotion that you felt like headbutting lampposts, or people - or both. Life was exciting but eventually the Teddy boy era slipped to one side, and smart Italian suits became the fashion, with short jackets and wider ties. As the Teddy days came to a sad end, drain pipe trousers were hung up to catch the rainwater of time, although there have been sightings of

Teds over the years, usually in places cut off from civilisation, like Glossop. (Only joking, Glossop.) Not so long ago I did see, as I drove through your wonderful town, a vision dressed in a drape jacket with a velvet collar, complete with the sideburns, wandering through the main street. Maybe it was a ghost?)

But at work I persevered, going through departments run by foremen who were all to be called Sir, by apprentices, until I came out of my time, as a skilled man. I finished up in a drawing office, at twenty three, where I learned to draw with a pencil, then with a pen, doing complicated plans of ship's gear boxes, which were made in the factory, then taken to ship yards like Harland and Wolf, and Cammell Laird. I stayed there four years or so, then moved on to other things, like building design, where things were made out of much warmer and friendly materials such as wood, and bricks, natural things, not with the cold impersonality of steel - things of the great outdoors such as trees and quarries.

Working at Metropolitan Vickers did so much for me, apart from the discipline - for which I am eternally grateful - including sending me to an Outward Bound school to learn mountain craft.

2   BEING GREEN IN ESKDALE GREEN

Four whole weeks away from the factory - it was a dream come true. No barking foreman. No riding on my Claude Butler bicycle with the alloy wheels, through dark mornings and between darker buildings, over hiding railway lines which were numerous, and which the alloy wheels would often come to grief with.

I can remember the excitement, on that train as it pulled into Seascale Station, excitement tinged with relief - and more than a touch of uncertainty. The station was already crowded with lads of my age group, all on the same mission as me, and more would come. On the station, a lad leant against a wall, and if ever a Teddy boy existed, it was this lad. Okay, he was minus the drape jacket, the luminous socks, drainpipe trousers, and all the other fine trappings of Teddy boy fashion, but he just had that aura. You see, us Teds just know these things. Like the Freemasons, but without the handshake. What he did have was the Brylcreamed Tony Curtis haircut, sideburns, the duck's arse at the back where the hair had been combed horizontally from both sides and then pointed downwards at the centre where the comb had formed a very straight vertical line. And the very way he leaned - I'd seen this lean a thousand times on Stretford Road, nonchalant and hard. The lad was wearing a green anorak but that didn't kid me. I knew he was a Ted. 'Hi, mate,' he greeted, before striking a match to light a cigarette. He was about an inch taller than I was but much broader. 'Where yer from?' said my new friend. 'Manchester,' I said. 'Thought as much,' said he, 'I'm from down the Smoke. Get me last ciggy before we start this performance.' I nodded and lit up myself. 'Mind you,' said he, 'If they think they're going to stop me smoking, they've another think coming, or getting a pint.' I nodded, blowing out smoke into the cool October air. Other trains pulled in, bringing young men from all over Britain, every one clutching at a variety of baggage and some looking like rats, scared at the sound of a barking dog. My friend and me looked on scornfully. We knew we were hard. I was from Hulme and my mate was from down the Smoke. 'Won't last a week, some of these wankers,' reflected my new pal. I nodded knowingly. I hoped I would.

Eventually the school instructors came. My pal from London, half way into his third cigarette, looked with contempt at the instructors, who herded us together like cattle.

A wimp appeared, about thirty years old, bespectacled, thin, frail looking. 'Follow us, please,' There was nothing wimpish about his voice. 'And you have your last drag for a month, then stub out your cigarette.' Those bespectacled eyes were focused on my newfound friend who glared back, blowing smoke in the instructor's direction. The instructor smiled - just, like a dentist with a mental problem before diving into your un-anaesthetised mouth with a faulty drill. On the bus to Eskdale, my mate told me that if that small specky four eyed bastard got in his way again, he was going to smack him. We'll call my new friend George, from now on. George was in for a shock.

At the Outward Bound School, we were assembled in a hall, and then formed into groups of ten or eleven boys to each patrol. The patrols were named after famous adventurers. I was in "Wilson" patrol, and so was my mate George. The original Wilson, I found out, was the doctor who was with the ill-fated South Pole expedition in which Scott died. Wilson also died - I hoped that it wasn't an omen. Other patrols were Shackleton, Scott, Tensing and others that I can't remember. All the patrols competed with each other for points that were totalled up at the end of the month. After a short briefing, we were introduced to our patrol instructor who then guided us to our dormitory, where we had to quickly change into something suitable for running up a hill - our first task. George said something about only coming here to write an article for his work's magazine, not racing up stupid hills in pissing rain. We, including George, gathered at the starting point. I think it was about three o'clock in the afternoon. There was a fine mist over the hills and it was drizzling. The instructor with the glasses, who was getting less wimpish by the second, told us that the last ten boys back would wash up for the whole school after the evening meal. George called him a very bad name, but quietly, because the instructor seemed to be looking constantly at my friend with that mad dentist look.

It didn't look a big hill. The top of it was the point where we had to turn back, and just to prove that we all got to the top, an instructor was there already, to check. In fact there were instructors all the way up the hill, to ensure that nobody cheated. Then we were off, up that

14

trail, a mixture of mud and rocks, a hundred young men - all not wanting to wash up for the school. The wimp instructor led the way, like a streak of greased lightening. 'Follow him,' shouted someone. A hundred lads followed and it was soon apparent just who was fit and who was not. Amazingly the hill had quadrupled in size, like magic. Everybody else but George was fitter than I was. Half way up my lungs were bursting and I was gasping noisily. Ninety eight lads seemed to be in front of me. George was behind. Three fifths of the way up, the bespectacled instructor was passing me going downwards. He looked calm, almost dancing over the rocks, like a gazelle. Then lads, a huge crowd, came charging down towards me, heading for home. Instructors shouted encouragement, reminding us about the washing up. I pushed myself, causing pain. My lungs couldn't cope and my legs needed muscles that did not exist. Then I was at the top where I turned. Going down I passed other lads on the way up. Where had they come from, I thought I was last. Some had stopped, including George who I thought had died. He was bent over with hands on his knees. His purple face dripped sweat and unhealthy sounds came from him, like a car makes when the cylinder-head gasket is badly damaged. I ran down, stumbling over a lad who had fallen on his way down. 'Get up,' shouted an instructor to the lad who was groaning and clutching a knee. I ran on, picking up speed and catching up on some of the lads. 'Well done,' said an instructor to me, 'That's the spirit.' At the end I collapsed in a heap, and there were heaps everywhere. George was not last, but nearly. Somebody started to identify the last ten lads, which included George. Then we had to stagger back to our dormitories, have a shower, and all meet again in the hall. The washing up had been a joke, but it worked, for me anyway.

The main building of the school was a solid and heavy looking mansion type of building called Gate House, with a spectacular view over a small lake then an horizon of mountains. It could not have been in a better location. We, Wilson patrol, were in an annex that had recently been built, a two-storey building of lakeland stone sides and a rendered frontage. We were downstairs with other groups upstairs. Other patrols slept elsewhere. Our annex looked out of place next to the main building. I was to recognise that building many years later when it featured in a film called 'She Was Wearing Pink Pyjamas' starring Julie Walters.

Our instructor was a slim, super fit guy, who read us the riot act that first day. He had an easy going approach to his job but would not suffer fools gladly, as we were to find out.

All the lads in our group got on well together other than a lad from London and me. It's funny isn't it, how people's chemistry does not always gel, and I knew that I disliked him right from day one. I also knew the feeling was mutual. From then on, we did everything in groups, either all eleven of us, or in smaller groups, after we had mastered our mountain-craft. Firstly we had to master knots, which we did by tying ropes around a pair of heavy looking stone gate posts, rock climbing, map reading, orienteering and just how to manage on ones own in an emergency. We even had tests on all these things, and were to be given points at the end that was to be represented by a small badge with different colours that depicted how we did. Thank God, there was no mathematics, singing or football. I still have that badge, something I'm very proud of, even if I did not do as well as some of the others.

The whole idea of that training was to push us to the point of no return, the point where we would normally have given up, just to prove to ourselves that we could go to greater lengths than we ever expected. At the time it seemed like a torture camp.

George had begun a hate campaign against the bespectacled instructor, and I with this guy I didn't like. Both were to prove pointless. One of our first walks, which was straight from the school, I believe was were you head north from Eskdale and after a few minutes, take a right where eventually you go through the woods of Mitterdale and up to the top of Whin Rig, which overlooks Wast Water, England's deepest and highest lake. We took the path that runs the length of Whin Rig then down to Burnmoor Tarn, just before the mighty Scarfell. I can't remember where we went from there, but what I do remember of that walk, was when one the lads, a very slightly built guy, fell at a stile. We had been really motoring and just reached the top of a hill, with the instructor leading. This lad was absolutely all in when he fell. George and I, being near the back, went to help the lad just as out instructor came running back from the lead to see what was the hold up. 'I can't go on', said the lad. 'Well, you'll stay here the night,' returned the instructor. 'Come on, leave him.' The instructor shot off, 'Come on'. I couldn't believe it was happening. Surely there was some law against all this.

'Bastard,' muttered George. I agreed, but we followed the instructor who whispered, 'Just keep your eyes on him, but don't let him know it.' We moved off, but looking back, we saw that the one who had fallen had got up and began to jog after us. The   instructor slowed his place and we noticed him occasionally looking back. The faller probably fell on more occasions during that month but never ever complained again. Like the instructor had said: 'You are only as fast as your slowest member,' and this lad was our slowest member, so we had to look after him.

Our first major length of time away from the school was a three day matter, with the instructor, where amongst other places, we went across Scarfell Pike. As everybody knows, Scarfell is England's highest mountain and one that is visited by thousands of walkers every year. I've since been up Scarfell many times by various routes and there have been so many people on the top, it resembled Piccadilly on a Saturday afternoon. But mid week, in October, in swirling mist and driving rain, there was nobody there but us lads and our instructor. How things can change in the Lake District. Any wonderful views of Wasdale were hidden by that grey mist and the wind got so bad we had at one point to crawl on all fours. Our instructor said that the wind had only got to seventy miles an hour but gusting at a hundred, so it was not so bad. Some of us were blown off our feet and I remember us clutching at a large rock for support. It was frightening, we couldn't breath properly, and we had to wait for about an hour for the wind to subside before we could continue. This was just not fun, and did I notice just a tinge of a worry line on the instructor's brow?

Another time, probably a four day affair, just before we were ready to go it without the instructor, our patrol firstly went through Mitterdale, past Burnmoor Tarn, then beyond the north end of Wast Water and then up to the hotel at Wasdale Head. An easy enough walk if it wasn't for the fact that I was carrying one of the large tents that slept six as well as my own gear. I felt like a yak, and probably looked like one. I remember motorists passing us on the road to the hotel, laughing at us from their insulated comfort. Some even offered us a lift. The object was to spend that first night, camping in Ennerdale which we could get to by following Black Sail Pass to the north of Kirk Fell.

As we passed the hotel, our instructor remarked that it was getting late and would be dark soon, so we had to get a move on. It was raining, as usual, as we made our way towards Black Sail Pass, with the darkness of Kirk Fell rising to our right and I remember that we had to cross a busy stream more than once. I was at the rear with George who was carrying the second tent and the main group were now out of sight ahead. Suddenly, our instructor shouted: 'You at the back, can you hear anything? Stop a minute.' We stopped and heard nothing but the wind and rushing stream waters, which was the usual sounds for that neck of the woods. Then, ears straining, a wailing noise not unlike the wind, filtered from our right. Then again and the wail had taken on a human voice sound. The wail became: 'Help! Is anybody there? Help!' The female voice was high pitched yet trailed off as if caught up in the wind and dragged away.

We shouted back. 'Hello, where are you?' Then, leaving our heavy baggage by the stream, began to make our way towards the cries for help. It was now darkening rapidly and as we climbed higher towards the sounds, the rain and wind intensified.

'Help. Over here. Help.' Voices get lost in the wind. We headed upwards. 'Help.'

'Where are you?'

Eventually, from the greyness, light coloured forms disengaged themselves from the rocks. They were human forms, and two in number. The human forms waved frantically. 'Over here, over here.'

I felt like saying 'Doctor Livingstone, I presume,' but there was not to be any humour.

'Oh, thank God you've found us,' the woman sobbed.

She was dressed in a skirt and the sort of coat she might have worn to go shopping in and she clutched a handbag tightly. The man had on a pac-a-mac, one of those plastic coats that you could roll up into a small ball and put in your pocket. Under that, he wore a suit with a shirt and tie and on his feet were the sort of shoes you would wear for the office. The woman had been crying. The man gulped and looked downwards guiltily. How on earth they had got that far wearing those clothes I will never understand.

'Stupid sod,' spat the woman to the man in the suit.

'I knew where I was,' lied the man. 'Just point me back to the stream, and I'll be alright.' The man had become smug. 'Take us back to the pub,' pleaded the woman.

'We can't,' I explained. 'We are late as it is. I'll show you to the stream and point you in the right direction.' The darkness was approaching rapidly and I was getting worried. 'How on earth have you got here?' I asked.

'I've got a map,' said the man, producing a beer mat from the hotel at Wasdale Head. The map was about three inches in diameter and useless as a map.

'Stupid man,' spat the woman. I mentally agreed.

The couple had come on a coach trip to Wasdale, from Liverpool, and he had decided to take her for a walk from the pub. We took them back to the stream and pointed in the direction of Wasdale Head and left them to it. They could not get lost if they followed the stream.

I often wondered how that couple managed to cross the stream, wearing those clothes especially the town shoes. Hopefully they managed to get back to the coach, but I reckon that he never took her on any more walks. We, George and myself, reckoned that this cretin had taken the woman up that hill with amorous motives, but I could not think of a more un-amorous setting than on the side of a severely windswept mountain in the driving rain.

That night we camped in Ennerdale. The instructor remarked that the ground was often soggy in Ennerdale. What he didn't say was that the ground was never not soggy. In the morning the ground sheets were six inches under water and our sleeping bags, and most other things, were soaked. From Ennerdale, on that second day, we walked over Hey Stacks, down Scarth Gap Pass and through Buttermere. From Buttermere, I haven't a clue where we went, but it rained constantly.

Eventually we would go in a large group, without the instructor, for a couple of days, taking it in turn to lead the patrol.

Other things we had to do included a course through the woods, which involved ropes, ladders and other means of getting yourself from A to B without your feet touching the ground, and then there was a twelve foot high wall that you all had to get over and be timed doing so. A certain idiot in lion skin trunks and a gurning chimpanzee for a pal would have breezed through it, but for city folk it was more of a challenge.

Once we went canoeing on Wast Water, and had to practice having to right your canoe from being upside down whilst hanging, head first in England's deepest waters. In the middle of Wast Water, looking down, all you see is an eerie and never ending blackness, and the water is freezing. We had to row to the Wasdale Head end of the water, and then race back, after which my hands were bleeding. I was glad to get back on dry land. but from the centre of Wast Water, the view is stunning, with the majestic but gloomy screes, a spectacular wall of fragmented rocks to one side, the steepness of Yewbarrow to the other, and Great Gable's predominant domed head to the front, overseeing everything. In Wasdale on a dull and rainy day it's as if you are totally hemmed in by an awesome presence, but like everything in the Lakes, the mood can change with the weather and in summer when the sun shines out of a clear blue sky, Wasdale takes on another character, when the greys become greens and even those dull fragmented screes become all shades of colour.

One day, one our few days off, a group of us were playing volleyball on the grass to the front of the main building, with some instructors watching. The guy I couldn't get on with, who had been winding me up for ages, was on the opposing team and at one point me and this guy clashed at the net. I can't remember what it was all about, but he was arrogant, I thought. He must have had the same feeling about me. Anyway punches were thrown by each of us, right through the net and the next minute instructors and other lads were separating us. 'There's a way to deal with this,' said one instructor, 'you can put on the gloves, and fight under boxing rules.' Which I thought was a good way to deal with it. However, I would have preferred to have had him a fight where rules included kicking, gouging, clubbing and strangulation. 'Okay,' I agreed. My opponent nodded, obviously also in agreement. Later though, things changed. They, the school authorities, decided on a better way to sort it out. We were coming up to the point where we, the lads, had to go out in pairs, on a given route, taking it in turn to lead, and the one not leading had to go along with the leader's decisions. They decided that me and my opponent would pair off for this treat under the assumption that we would come back the best of friends after three days of relying on each other. I didn't fancy the idea, but we both agreed to the scheme.

We were given certain map references and place names where we had to be at certain times of the day. On the first night we were to camp at a place called Three Tarns. My opponent was leading at the time but I was checking on my map. We had already had a few minor rows by then as I had disagreed with his direction finding and it was getting late. We were at the time when we should be near to Three Tarns, a place named, obviously, after the three tarns that are close together near the path - Lakeland people are not stupid. We had walked up from Eskdale and Three Tarns was just before the top of Bow Fell. It was darkening and in another hour I reckoned we would have to use our torches, when he suddenly stated; 'This is it,' pointing to three pools of water resembling large puddles. I swore with great enthusiasm at his stupidity.

'Oh, don't start,' said he, 'this is where we camp for the night.'

I was tired and really wanted to bed down for the night, but these pools were definitely not tarns. In fact in dryer times they would probably not have be there, never mind be a permanent fixture on the map. If we lost an hour tonight we would only have to add an hour on tomorrow, an impossible task. I set my compass and carried on.

'You'll get in trouble for this,' he shouted as I marched on. 'We are not supposed to separate. And I'm leading.'

'Not anymore,' shouted I.

Fifteen minutes later, three obvious tarns appeared and I was relieved. Eventually, he caught up, embarrassed but saying nothing. We bivouacked up for the night, I think against the dry stone wall of a sheep enclosure, and I don't think we spoke hardly for the remaining time on that hike. I don't think we spoke again for that matter, ever. When we got back to the school, the instructors were amazed that we had not become friends. I wasn't.

The days when we were not up in the mountains, always began by some idiot blowing a horn to wake everybody up. I think this was at about half past six. Then we all had to run around the lake by the path that skirted it. At its furthest point, there was a small waterfall that fed water into the lake. At the waterfall we had to jump into the freezing water, one at a time, while an instructor operated a device that was like a sliding wooden door which he lifted when sufficient water had gathered to drench us. If our hair had not got wet, we were chucked back in. The person who invented this little perversion must have had a serious mind problem. Now I reckon that even in the height of summer, that water would have been bloody cold, but in October it was freezing. After that we would run back to our dormitory, shower and be ready for the day. I hated those mornings.

Once, with all of our patrol and the instructor, on a four-day hike, I developed a large red sided boil on my leg near the knee. It had blown up suddenly and resembled mount Etna just before the damage. Half way through this day, I was cringing with pain at every step, and the boil looked as sore as it was.

'You can't walk with that,' said the instructor, with a concern that amazed me, and I was to get off the mountain and wait at a road junction at a certain time to be picked up by someone. Then, at the appointed time, this car pulled up and the school doctor took me back to the school. The timing was immaculate. I was led into the first aid room and the school nurse took one look at my leg, and said scornfully: 'We'll soon have that sorted out, my boy. It's nothing, that.' I mentally disagreed while she put the kettle on and cleaned out a milk bottle. I was intrigued and in pain. 'We'll suck it out,' said she, eventually, pouring boiling water into the bottle. I thought she meant with her mouth, she looked the type. The nurse smiled like a torturer, clutching the hot bottle wrapped in a towel. I gulped as the bottle neared my boil. 'Don't move,' ordered the Marquis de Sade in drag, clamping the neck of the bottle over the largest boil I've ever known. I used an 'F' word as she gripped my leg and pressed the hot bottle neck on to my raw skin. 'Mardy bugger,' spat the bitch, enjoying every minute of my pain. As the steam condensed, causing a vacuum, a large lump of pus shot into the bottle. I thought about fainting, but that would have been an easy way out. The nurse from hell grinned, needing to subject me to a lot more pain and held up the bottle, nodding happily at its contents, which was most of my leg. I stared down at the gaping hole and redness, but the swelling was gone. Then the nurse cleaned the wound with the delicate touch of someone who digs roads for a living and then bandaged her handiwork, hiding it from the authorities. Then she made me a cup of tea and I wondered what was in it.

22

As I sat there, one of the instructors came in with a massive wound on his lower leg. He had been in a fell race and had fallen- maybe that's why they call them fell races - badly gashing his leg, just above the ankle. A large piece of flesh flapped loosely over his sock. 'That's nasty,' said the nurse with unknown compassion in her voice but not in her expression.

'I'll see to it,' said the man. Then I watched in amazement as the instructor, a trainee doctor, cleaned his horrible wound and then proceeded to stitch the loose flesh back to his leg during which, he did not flinch once. The nurse looked on appreciatively, until he got up and vacated the first aid room without saying a word.

'And you're moaning about your bit of a boil,' spat the nurse. 'Finish your tea and scram. You'll be back on the fells tomorrow.' Unbelievable people, these. I wanted to go home.

It was a day or two before the end and we had to do some final tests, some of them before invited guests, families of the staff and some people who lived in Eskdale. It was supposed to be a fun day - for the guests, not us. I forget what all the games were but one was jousting on the lake, in pairs canoes. I was with my mate George. I think we had to ram our opponents with brushes and try to tip them into the water. George and I won our joust with our opponents ending up in the lake. Now, my mate George always wore a large leather belt with a massive metal buckle. After we had brought our canoe on to dry land, we had to walk through a group of instructors and other people. One of the instructor's wives said to him: 'What's that stupid belt for?' I think she was the wife of the wimp who wasn't a wimp, and I harboured a deep feeling it was all planned to humiliate George in front of people. 'It holds my trousers up, luv,' explained George casually, making his way through the crowd.

Also, during those last few days, we had to perform a stage act in front of staff and villagers, in the hall, doing whatever we wanted. We in Wilson patrol did a little song and dance act with me as the Emcee. We made a musical instrument out of ten bottles filled to different levels with water. When we tapped the bottles with a ruler we created a tune - of sorts - and we sang:

'Does your chewing gum lose its flavour on the bivouac over night,
If your mother says don't chew it do you swallow it in spite?.'

Actually, the rest of the patrol sang - I introduced the act and wrote the song. (By changing the words of Lonny Donagon's original words) The audience roared their approval and we won that contest. Overall, we didn't do too badly and I personally was pleased with my performance and the marks I got.

After that month, I reckon any of us could survive on a mountain, without rations and in most conditions. I also reckon I could find my way, with map and compass, to most places within reasonable reach. I also know that I was in the fittest condition of my life. I remember going home, though, hating those mountains, tarns, and country things - not least streams that had to be jumped into naked. On the train home, I vowed never to hike or put myself through such pain ever again.

3   BACK TO WORK

I was eighteen, a Teddy boy, engaged to be married, fit as a butcher's dog and learning a trade. I returned to work after that month in the Outward-Bound School, full of it all. My department looked a sorry sight after the Lakeland hills - which I harboured a grudge against for a couple of years- but life had to go on. Trafford Park, during the rush hour was madness, with thousands of bikes and a never-ending stream of buses bringing people to and from work. I remember lots of fog and evil smog, when Trafford Park and most of Manchester had disappeared as I rode to work. But I was going nowhere, just to and from work, and Stretford Technical College, where I was struggling.

Our supervision started with chargehands who gave us our work, who reported to foremen who disciplined us and sometimes were disciplined by general foremen who looked up to the almighty superintendents, the Gods of the departments who sometimes we never saw until they'd be there with some important visitors looking around the factory. The workers despised the chargehands, hated the foremen and were shit scared of the superintendents. Everybody had a place and everybody knew it. Over it all were the unions, and at the bottom of the pile were the apprentices which included me. If you wanted to escape, you would have to pass your exams at technical college and then maybe get into a drawing office, or some other such higher plane that seemed to float a million miles above your grasp. The thing at eighteen was to get to be twenty-one in one piece and then become fully skilled at your chosen craft.

The years passed by, and it was only gradually that I overcame the hate for the hills, realising that I would actually enjoy putting into practice what I had learned at the Outward Bound School. I began to venture out again to the hills local to Manchester, mainly around the Pennines and mostly on my own.

At about twenty four I met my first long standing hiking pal at work. By this time I'd made the break and was working in a drawing office. I was by then married with a growing family, and living in a council house in Wythenshawe - probably Europe's largest garden council estate. Trees, grass and green things were everywhere. People had gardens, which some of them tended and produced much colour. Some didn't. Manchester Airport was round the corner and sometimes aeroplane fuel vapour filled the air. The rented house we had to leave in Hulme - because all those houses were being demolished in order to build the new Hulme - had been painted internally with a vile and sickly yellow throughout and didn't have a bath. The toilet, which froze up in winter, was in an out-building in the back yard.

The house in Woodhouse Park, Wythenshawe, was luxury, with a toilet that didn't freeze, a bath and a gas fire in the living room.

Frank had had an upbringing something like mine, living in Rusholme, which was not far from my first school, Princess Road, so he and I hit it off straight away. We started to go out for drinks together and then for a curry after, during which we would usually put the world to rights. I'm not ashamed to say we had some momentous drinking sessions during which we cured every problem known to man. We had similar thoughts on things, such as conservation, and we very soon became the best of pals. Frank also had an amazing ability to be sick in the most obscure places, a skill for which he eventually became a legend, and he was also interested in hiking. The two sometimes combined.

At first our hikes were in Derbyshire, where we usually started from Hayfield or Edale, and we explored places that I had not been to before. And Frank was a lot fitter than me, in spite of the fact that at the time he smoked cigarettes, even whilst hiking

. Once, I remember, Frank and I walked to Edale from Hayfield, and had about five pints in a pub there, then hiked back, peeing frequently, Frank smoked there and back.. I was knackered, especially going back up Jacob's Ladder on our return to Hayfield, carrying five pints inside me. I think we celebrated getting up Jacob's Ladder by peeing from the top of it. We also walked from Edale up Grindsbrook, which is one way of starting the Pennine Way (and probably the best part of it) a lovely walk, especially if you follow the stream and scramble up the waterfalls to the top where peat bogs prevail. Now, Frank had a belief, like mine, that people should not pollute the hills by wearing anything that was not green coloured, mind you in those days fell walking was not the designer label industry it is today so people then did not have the wide range of colours and breathable fabrics available now. Frank also firmly believed that the hills belonged to him alone and maybe the odd hiker in green. Once we camped on the camp site at Wasdale Head and on the first night in the pub there, we each had ten bottles of Newcastle Brown ale and some glasses of whisky, which we drank whilst sitting on the floor in a corridor. When it was time to get up and go, we couldn't stand properly and then after managing to stagger out, we both fell into the privets near the hotel front. Frank was sick into those privets. Some people saw our condition, and feeling sorry for us gave us a lift in a Land Rover. Not much later, after struggling into our sleeping bags, we made the stupid plan to get up early and jump into Wast Water.

In the morning, I knew from waking that we had made a mistake with our plans. It was freezing cold and the hills, including Scarfell, which we had planned to climb later, were hiding behind mist, and greys were everywhere. On mornings like that Wasdale looks very eerie with an almost haunting gloom. One could almost imagine some evil presence, like a banshee drawing one into those deep black waters, to be sucked under and never to be seen again. It's worse with a hangover from hell.

'This will cure us,' said Frank, as we ran through the cold fine drizzle between the tents of the campsite and to the water's edge. Frank was first into the water and I heard him scream as I jumped in. I screamed too. It was not the monster from the lake that got us but the freezing water. I couldn't breathe and thought I was going to die in that gloomy lake. Frank was right about one thing, though, it did cure our hangover, probably by anaesthetising it, although I'd rather have my hangover back than die of hypothermia. 'Bloody fools,' said someone strolling by, an intelligent man. We were out of that water as fast as possible and back to our tent from where we cooked a good breakfast of bacon, sausages and beans. Soon the wonderful smell of bacon frying over numerous primus stoves filled the air as hungry campers got ready for a day on the fells. Campsites wouldn't be campsites without that famous aroma and in Wasdale that smell filtered across to the road as a sign to other people that the place was inhabited and all was not gloom. The smell of bacon frying is also a deterrent to malignant forces such as banshees and creatures from black lagoons.

The path up to Scarfell was already dotted with walkers, not all in green I might add, Frank and myself made our way from the camp site and started the ascent through Brown Tongue, which was named after a foreman at Metropolitan Vickers who used to spend his weekends cleaning the superintendent's car. Looking up we could see the rear ends of many people disappearing into a mist that was clearing rapidly. Reds, blues and yellows polluted the path but we, in green, blended into the hillside and became part of it. The path got steeper, much steeper than when I'd done it at eighteen with the Outward Bound School. Maybe they'd altered it? Frank led and the distance between us widened as the steepness increased. My breathing became laboured and I stopped a few times to wheeze great breaths as Frank disappeared from view. Reds blues and yellows - and the odd green-passed me, effortlessly but polluting the mountain. Burping, I brought up some liquid that tasted of my breakfast mainly because it was my breakfast. But I plodded on, upwards into the mist that had become wisps of whitish greys. The sweat on my face was cooled by the fine rain and the wind felt like heaven.

Somewhere before the top, I spied Frank sitting on a rock, the smoke from his cigarette making a union with the mist. He waited for me to catch up, and then we reached for Scarfell Pike together to witness the ultimate sacrilege at the Pike. It looked like a multi-coloured football crowd covering that famous place, like a swarm of bees that had been dipped into rainbow paint. 'Bastards,' spat Frank, as we veered left, not even bothering to join that mass of human beings on the Pike. We headed left, going over Broad Crag then down to the path that runs from Angle Tarn to Sty Head Tarn. My breakfast jumped up and down on the steep bits as my knees jolted with every step. Then, would you believe it, the mist disappeared and the sun appeared in a blue sky as we reached Sprinkling Tarn where we rested and Frank had a cigarette. We sat by the water's edge as Frank blew smoke out while cursing those multi-coloured morons and the sun for being late. We stayed at Sprinkling Tarn for ages, talking then just resting and I think I fell asleep for a while before Frank woke me up to continue. The views as we reached Sty Head were spectacular in the bright sunlight, with the moon-rocky slope of Great Gable to our right and Wasdale to the front. Walking back to the valley with both of us sweating, Wastwater looked inviting ahead, inviting enough to jump into we commented.

We ziz-zagged down to the lower path then followed the stream then past the little church and, on to the pub. The sun was still bright in that blue sky and, sweating profusely, I followed Frank as his pace increased and he reached the pub thirty paces before me. As I entered the bar he was watching the pints being poured, with his tongue hanging from an open mouth and his eyes bulged like a dog on heat. Frothy golden liquid cascaded down my throat with the speed of a waterfall, sending a shiver down my spine and a wonderful feeling throughout as the alcohol took root, cooling my body and relaxing my brain. Then we ordered two more pints, just to be sure. These we took outside and drank leisurely while sitting on a wall.

The hikes with Frank were numerous over probably a six year period and I cannot remember exactly the order of them all. Firstly we had many hikes over the Pennines of Derbyshire, then a few long weekends in the lakes. I think that Wasdale trip was one of our first trips to the Lakes, and I picked that one because I knew the area well.

Once, before Frank bought a car, we must have got the train to Windermere, not having any specific plans, but carrying a tent and all the gear for camping. On the first day, feeling peckish and thirsty, we wandered into a pub in Grasmere. We then planned later to climb up The Old Pack Horse Road and camp for the night by Grisedale Tarn, and be ready the next day to head north over Helvellyn and then maybe drop down again by Thirlmere, or wherever we fancied. It was about two o'clock in the afternoon and I ordered a pint of bitter with some soup. Frank had a pint of Guinness and a bowl of Irish Stewed Steak to cure his hunger pangs. My soup was delicious and I savoured the beer that I sipped patiently, but Frank on the other hand, had gone quite, having supped most of his Guinness and began to linger over his meal. Also he had gone a funny grey colour, the opposite from his usual ruddy complexion. He downed his remaining Guinness, wiped his mouth and said: 'I'll have to get some fresh air.' Then without waiting for a reply, got up and made for the exit door. I followed him into the fresh lakeland air of the afternoon. Facing the pub was a farm on the other side of the road, and on the pavement next to the garden of the farmhouse was a timber form on which we both sat. Frank had gone a deathly white and was breathing in great gasps of cooling air. Then he turned, away from the road, to be sick.

In the farmhouse garden, amongst the flowers and shrubs, there was a little lamb. A cute little thing, all scrubbed and white, and looked more a domestic pet, more so because of its apparent friendliness to human beings. Baa, said the little lamb, begging attention, approaching the low dry stone wall between us and it. 'Uggggg,' said Frank in reply, covering the friendly face and pleading eyes of his new friend with stewed steak and a full pint of Guinness. The stewed steak now had a predominance of lamb in its recipe, that would not go away. The bright little eyes peered through the potatoes and carrots and black liquid dripped from its once white wool. Frank burst out laughing, dribbling out the remains of his meal. The lamb stayed its ground, a walking casserole, wanting to be petted. Of course, Frank uttered the classic: 'I don't remember eating that,' before we hurried from the spot, crying with laughter.

Not much later, we approached the start of The Old Pack Horse Road from the main road, still laughing. The Old Pack Horse Road is really nothing more than a fairly steep path that leads directly to Grisedale Tarn from the main road. The hillside below the path is known as Great Tongue, which, said Frank is, exactly what is needed to clean up that little lamb, We laughed all the way up that hill, but our laughing subsided when we reached our intended camping site, the flattish ground that surrounds Grisedale Tarn. The weather had changed rapidly and heavy rain came from nowhere. The tent went up quicker than ever and soon we were under cover, sheltered from the elements, but worried as great gusts of wind shuddered against the canvas. We placed large rocks over our guy ropes and attempted to weigh everything down, which before morning we were to find had failed. Cooking was a nightmare and I think we ate cold beans from the tin, which Frank said was better than the stewed steak in Grasmere. That little sheep would have gone down a treat, he added. Especially now that it was marinated in Guinness.

The night was a total disaster, during which I don't think we slept for more than an hour or so, as the wind intensified and the rain lashed our tent, which did not benefit from having a sewn-in ground sheet. The tent pegs were dragged from the ground and the guy ropes pulled from the ballast of rocks, leaving me and Frank hanging on to the canvas for dear life. Eventually we gave up, with the tent now wrapped around us and our gear all blown about the tarn-side by the freak wind. Frank's jacket and some other clothing was never seen again and by the break of daylight, the place looked like a battlefield. Collecting our belongings and clearing up the place was hard work but by morning the wind had died down although it was still raining a fine drizzle. Needless to say, we were not in the mood to go on over Helvellyn, especially as none of our clothing was dry and we were red eyed with lack of sleep. After collecting our sodden goods, we headed straight back down The Old Pack Horse Road with the intention of getting to Windermere from where we would get a train straight back to Manchester.

Approaching Windermere station, with rucksacks full of soggy clothing, we were informed that there was not a train to Manchester for another few hours. Frank and I had a meeting of two and voted to stay the night in or near Windermere if we could find a place to put up what remained of our tent. But we went for a pint first, determined to get something sensible to eat, knowing that stewed steak was out of the question. Later we climbed a low hillside from the town, through some woods, finding ourselves in a little clearing protected on one flank by the trees. We set up camp there and Frank created a washing line upon which he hung some of his wet clothes, which included his sodden white underpants which fluttered in the breeze. Not in the mood for much talking, we fell asleep early and deeply, sleeping through until an untimely awakening in the morning.

The man with a shotgun was pulling at Frank's underpants and swearing.

'Get off my underpants,' said Frank, peering from the tent.

'And you get off this land,' replied the farmer. A black and white sheepdog glared into the tent and the business end of the double barrelled gun waved over Frank's head 'I'm not allowed to have people camping on this land. The landlord will have my hide for this.'

'Well, give us time,' pleaded Frank.

'No,' said the man. 'Get off my farm.' 'We were wet through,' I explained. 'These are dry' now,' said the farmer feeling Frank's underpants thoroughly. 'So get gone.'

'How did you know we were here?' asked Frank.

I could see your underpants fluttering in the breeze from the farmhouse window,' explained the farmer. 'I'll give you ten minutes, then be gone.'

'Bastard,' spat Frank as the man and his dog walked back down the hill to the farmhouse that was now visible in the morning light. Later, with rucksacks full of a mixture of wet and dry clothes, we boarded the train back to Manchester.

Some months later, Frank informed me that the police had been in touch with him regarding clothes and other personal belongings that had been found washed up by Grisedale Tarn with one of the items bearing his details. The police, having searched the tarn for a body, were going to take proceedings against him for wasting their time, but just gave him a warning instead.

Another time, at Easter, Frank and I decided to go to camp near Keswick with the intention of investigating Skiddaw and the surrounding area, a place I was not at the time familiar with. Again someone had been doing a rain dance very successfully. This was the late sixties or maybe early seventies when hippies were still the rage, and to prove it Keswick was full of them, and bikers. On that first day, Good Friday you could not move without banging into long haired, bearded peace freaks and scruffy bikers. It was like a convention of the great unwashed, literally thousands of them, who had taken over the streets of Keswick. Two policemen tried to keep order and failed with the shear numbers involved. Frank and I fought our way through the matted hair, medallions, bedrolls and smell, to finish up at a campsite at Castlerigg, a mile or so south east of the town where our feet sank three inches into the damp ground. We erected our tent in a fine drizzle knowing we were a mile or so from the smell, then made our way back along the A591 to begin our ascent of Skiddaw. Skiddaw can appear a wonderful sight on sunny days but when it's drizzling under grey skies, it is a bleak prospect, especially the higher you get, when slippery slates prevail. We began the walk from the main road but I can't remember which path, then walking up, still on a tarmac road, we passed a farm where an old man sat on a bench near the farmhouse entrance.

'Morning,' greeted Frank.

'Mornin',' returned the old man, 'not so nice is it?'

'No,' agreed Frank. 'Is this the way to Skiddaw?'

'What's Skiddaw?' asked the man.

'The mountain, Skiddaw,' said Frank. 'Is this the way up?'

'Wouldn't know,' said the man, frowning. 'I aint never been any further than these gates. Let me know what you find when you come back.'

When we were out of earshot, Frank said: 'Piss off, he's having us on.'

Well it was the way up to Skiddaw, and to prove it we eventually got on the mountain top, a walk we did without meeting one of the smelly brigade who were all humming together in Keswick. The only people we did encounter on the way up was a group of elderly walkers, one of whom explained that he was eighty four, and walked every weekend, a fact that endorsed Frank's belief that walking up mountains is the best exercise ever, especially when combined with drinking vast amounts of Newcastle Brown. The old ones were dressed in green.

On the top of Skiddaw, apart from the bleak view and the rain, we were met with a strange sight. A man, elderly and bearded, was on his hands and knees, picking at the small rocks on the ground, studying them through spectacles which perched on the end of his long nose.

'Lost something?' asked Frank.

'No, found something?' replied the strange man, holding up what looked like a small rock fragment. .'This place is littered with fossils.'

'I'm looking at one of them,' said Frank under his breath.

'Crustaceans that were once on the sea bed,' explained the man, beaming at his catch.

We left the man to his fossils as the rain intensified. Looking back on the descent, we could see the man, still on his hands and knees, searching. A fossil looking for fossils.

It rained all the way back. Frank had intended saying something rude to the old man who professed not to know about Skiddaw, but the man was not there as we passed the farm. Back at Castlerigg, the campsite was awash, but the rain had ceased. I can't remember what we had for our evening meal, but whatever it was, was cooked on the primus stove and devoured hungrily before we made our way to the pub, the Twa Dogs Hotel, which was not far away. The pub was crowded with hikers and some of the bikers had also ventured there. I think we had to sit on the pavement outside where we drank until late and put the world to right again, something Frank and I were good at. Later staggering back down the unlit country lane Frank scolded me for flickering my torch on and off. Other torch wielding campers joined us, all heading for the tents and another night to remember --or forget. If the rain by Grisedale Tarn had been bad then this was worse. It began probably an hour after we had nodded off, when the machine gun sound of the rain on canvas woke us up and everybody else on the site. In spite of our alcoholic intake, we were not to sleep again that night, and neither was anybody else at Castlerigg - thunder, lightning and rain from hell saw to that. Again we hung on to the tent as it poured down and the ground under us got wetter until it resembled a foot thick lake of black porridge that we sank into. Cursing and swearing filled the air and some people packed up in the early hours of the morning. We looked out to see people struggling helplessly to dismantle tents that flapped about under lightning filled skies and driving rain that would not let up. We were made of sterner stuff, Frank and I, but only just. We stuck it out until morning when the campsite looked as if a bomb had hit it and just a few tents remained upright. Tired and weary campers wandered about looking like lost souls in hell, their boots squelching in the soggy ground. A man in a caravan smiled from his sheltered home at the devastation and Frank called him a bastard.

Again we packed up wet things, vowing never to return to that place. Eventually we headed back up the start of Skiddaw to a flat place by a stream that was sheltered on two side by trees and surrounded by a fence, where we erected what remained of the tent, and where we cooked breakfast so that the smell of bacon could fend off any bad spirits that might have been hanging around in the trees. After that the sun came out and we slept for hours, making up for the sleep we had missed. Alas, our dreams were shattered about mid-day by the sound of angry voices that coincided with the tent being shaken violently. 'Get out,' shouted a voice that invaded my dreams. Frank cursed and stuck his head out of the tent. My head joined his.

Three angry men and one angry dog looked down at us, but the bright sun blurred my vision as I looked up. 'If you're not gone from here within ten minutes,' said one of the men, 'you'll be heavily fined. This is Water Board land.' 'So piss off,' said another.' 'We'll be back,' said a third, 'with the police.'

'We're not doing any harm,' explained Frank.

'It's up to you,' said a Water Board official. The men and dog moved off, leaving us to our packing. After that we gave up, vowing to give up camping forever.

Frank's ability to be sick at any given moment was always a source of amusement and the stuff of many stories. Once, we were in a famous Indian restaurant in the centre of Manchester, having a vindaloo each. Frank cleared his plate and then, without warning, brought everything back, filling the bowl used for the curry sauce. The bowl filled to the brim. The waiter approached, enquiring as to how we had enjoyed our meal. Wonderful said Frank. I nodded in agreement. 'Why haven't you eaten it?' asked the waiter.

'Oh, I have,' said Frank, as the frowning waiter removed the bowls from the table.

4   THE PROLIFIC TIME

During my late twenties and most of my thirties I put in more fell walking hours than ever, getting to know the Derbyshire Pennines and certain areas of the Lake District like the back of my hand. Metropolitan Vickers, that became AEI, then GEC, was a thing of my past. 27,000 people had been employed at "Metrovicks" during it's heyday, but the numbers were now dwindling as manufacturing generally was on a steady decline in this country. Trafford Park was changing too, and many of those railway lines became redundant and some removed forever.

Alan Rayner became my next long term hiking mate. I was nearly thirty and he was still an apprentice when we first met at work. From day one, he had this inquisitiveness about the hills, that still holds firm with him to this day and looking back, we had some wonderful times exploring the fells. Alan had, and has still got, very solid, strong legs, a phenomenal gift for snoring, and is pretty fearless in most situations.

We spent the first few years going around the Pennines and The Lake District, and on one occasion, with another workmate Peter Glyn, we decided to stay at Brothers Water in the Lake District, staying for a couple of nights in the Brothers Water Hotel, just before Patterdale. Our main aim was to go up the famous Striding Edge ridge walk to the top of Helvellyn, weather permitting. On the Saturday, we got there early so we did a small walk over the path that runs to the west of Brothers Water, walking south then going up over Dovedale then up to Hart Crag at the highest point. It was an easy walk, in good conditions, with a good view into Patterdale and over the road to Harstsop Dodd. The hills were white with snow and the air was crisp and good to walk in. We got back to have a good meal and a lot to drink before getting to bed. Thankfully, I shared a room with Peter Glyn and avoided Alan's snoring, so I thought. In the night I could hear Alan's snoring shuddering through two bedroom doors. Alan has a brother call Les, who can snore louder. You'll meet Les later, in Iceland. I think the Rayner brothers share a genetic fault which turns the nostrils into a speedway motorbike during the hours of darkness.

The next day was perfect for the intended walk. Bits of blue sky peeped between the whites and greys of the clouds that must be there to give the lake District that certain awesome quality. And visibility was excellent as we approached the path up from Patterdale. Lots of snow could be seen on the high parts especially to our right towards Eagle Crag. Quite a few walkers were on the hills, especially on the way up to Striding Edge, which is common for most parts of the year. As we approached Hole-in-the-Wall, we could see that the northern slope down to Red Tarn was covered with snow, a scary sight, bearing in mind that the other side of the Edge was virtually without snow, as if another world had opened up to the north. Striding Edge as everybody knows, is a bit of a Mecca for hikers. It's one of those places that everybody has done at some stage of their hiking life. For those who don't know, Striding Edge, is a wonderful ridge walk to be done in good weather only. The famous Wainwright regarded Striding Edge as the finest Ridge walk in England, which is an accolade from a great authority in these matters. Traversing the edge is an experience to be savoured, with steep drops most of the time to both sides, to the north, that day looking down the snowy incline to Red Tarn and to the steep wastes to the south. Looking ahead, Helvellyn was a blanket of snow. The pointed ridge as you climb up seems to be too steep and pointed to be climbed, as if you would fall off without something to hold on to. But it's deceptive and many booted feet before have left an obvious way up, some of the time.

This day, a bloke with a big Alsation dog was ahead of us, and the dog was whining loudly as the man tried to drag the poor thing up and over the steep and jagged rocks on the top of the ridge. The dog was scared to death, and definitely did not want to go further, as it was trying to tell its owner. It had more sense than its master, who tugged at the dog's lead like an idiot, scolding the dumb mutt who wasn't as dumb as its master. But eventually the dog gave up and thankfully refused to budge. It sat defiantly staring at its master, with its mouth open from which a huge tongue waved in the cold air.

'Take it back,' ordered Alan to its master, as we passed the defiant animal. He also called the man a word you don't often come across on Striding Edge.

But this had unnerved Peter. We were at a very tricky part of the ridge in a sort of a small col between two steep bits and the views to the side were extremely steep down.

'I can't go on,' said Peter, looking as if a dizzy spell was taking him over.

'No problem,' said Alan. 'If you can get back on your own to where this path meets the one back to Red Tarn, then turn along that path and you can wait for us at the tarn.'

Peter agreed and went back, a task that he would be able to handle. We watched as he climbed down, passing the man with the dog. Eventually Alan and myself got to the top of Helvellyn, where a six inch mattress of snow prevailed, and many people gathered as if waiting for an open air church Mass. The views were terrific, especially the one looking back along Striding Edge with its Red Tarn side covered in snow. As I write, I'm looking at a photograph of that view which I took that day. A few dark rocks project up through the snow on that drop towards Red Tarn, to the left, and to the right, just smatterings of snow cling to a lower path. Beyond, the sun brightens the top of the fells beyond Patterdale, and snow covers the tops like icing on a cake.

Knowing we had to meet Peter, we did not linger and headed north along the path that would eventually meet the one going east over Swirral Edge and down to the tarn. Peter was asleep on the path near the tarn, and snoring, so we joined him and also fell asleep, but the noise of Alan 's snoring woke us both, so we had to continue back.

That night, back at The Brothers Water Hotel, we had a meal. I think I had a curry, followed by lots of beer. We were sitting in a corner of the restaurant and I think we were the only diners. In another part of the room there was a convention going on, of people - I use the term loosely - who all had various brain malfunctions. Around a pool table were some convention members, scruffy bikers (who didn't have bikes, by the way) in leathers who were noisy but not bothering us. I think they were camping near by or in a hostel near the hotel. One of them, a scrawny, white faced individual shouted frequently and obscenely at everybody and swung a pool cue viciously over his head. He also danced on the pool table. His mates laughed, obviously just as retarded. There must have been fifteen of them.

'Hope he doesn't come over here,' remarked Alan.

The leathered retarded ones noticed us looking at them and then the main idiot came dancing towards us, grinning like the fool he was, and swinging his pool cue around his head. Now Peter, the quietest of us, had his back to all of this, but Alan and myself feared the worst. The pool cue end touched Peter's head, and then rolled on to the top of his head, while the idiot made silly remarks and laughed. The fourteen looked across from the pool table, all smirking, waiting to see what would happen. Some stood menacingly, hands on hips. I gripped a loose stool by my side, ready if an onslaught came. Peter said nothing, but Alan leaned forward, beckoning the one with cue, who stooped over and near to Alan. 'If you don't go away off with that cue, I'm going to insert it into one of your body orifices, all of it,' said Alan quietly. No, he didn't say that exactly, what he said meant the same but was a thousand times more forceful and was littered with swear words. The retarded one understood because they were words from his own dictionary - a book of one page. His face went blank then he grinned and returned to his mates, who, listened then glared over to us. The largest one of them, a really hard looking character who looked as if he'd done a couple of rounds with Sonny Liston and lost every second of them, led the way. The motley crew following, smirking.

'I believe that you're going to shove the cue up my mate's arse?' asked the man, quietly and pan faced, staring Alan in the eyes. He folded his Bluto arms, waiting an answer.

Alan nodded. 'That's correct.'

The man leant forward and it seemed ages before he spoke. 'Well, you won't have to,' said the big man, 'cos I'm gonna do it for you. I'm sorry about my stupid mate.' With that he turned and pushed his pal to the floor, 'Now fucking apologise.' The scrawny man stood up and said 'Sorry,' meekly, before being led back to the pool table, from where he did not utter another word. My grip on the stool relaxed and we all breathed a sigh of relief, pursuing our night of drinking without further incident.

I must have had a lot to drink that night because I didn't hear Alan's snoring. Peter said in the morning I'd tried to pee in his wardrobe, something I did on another occasion at the *Sportsman* in Hayfield.

The next day we did a little hike somewhere then returned home in Alan's car. Before leaving the Hotel, we saw the bikers outside getting ready to leave. The one who had caused the trouble looked sheepish when he saw us looking at him, and he turned away. The big man just laughed and packed away his gear.

5   LAND OF FIRE AND NO BEER

Half the battle, when hiking is to find somebody to go with, someone who is fit, knows about mountaineering, and also knows when to keep quiet when words are not needed. Alan Rayner fitted the bill perfectly. I don't like going in large groups and all of my walking mates had that certain something that made them enjoyable companions on the fells. A total appreciation of what it's all about and the obvious sense of humour, especially if things go slightly wrong, which often they did. Sometimes, even sitting on the top of Mount Famine, a little peak just outside Hayfield, looking over to Kinder, on a weekday with not a soul in site, can be the most rewarding experience, feeling the quiet and knowing that nobody will interrupt your thoughts. Just the odd bird high in the sky for company and the sight of a young horse playing in a field below. I suppose this is called contemplation, but I'm sure that it doesn't suit everyone.

I've got mates who would never climb a mountain, and not even venture a half mile from their cars on a sunny day. But that's them, and they are entitled to their views.

I can remember one New Year's Eve, in Failsworth. (We bought a house there in 1973) We were at a party with some neighbours and it was about four o'clock in the morning when some absolutely drunken idiot, not me, suggested going for a hike the next day, well that day to be precise. 'Good idea,' I slurred. 'We'll go up Kinder from Hayfield.'

'Don't you make some stupid decisions when under the influence.'

In the morning the weather was the kind that you would always advise other people never to go hiking in., absolutely terrible. But we, four of us, ventured to Hayfield and I led them up Kinder from the car park, and up to the west of Kinder Low on to the path that leads to the Downfall. Visibility was a thing of the past. The higher we got, the worse got the weather, and the rain turned to sleet which turned to snow and the well worn path got boggier, not an unusual occurrence on Kinder. Then the wind blew in gale force proportions, and it was freezing cold. Getting to the Downfall was a nightmare, with us all nearly being blown off the hillside. Then passing the Downfall, where it's always windy, we could hardly move or see anything in the driving snow and mist. Some of them, not as well prepared as myself

40

were wet through, numb with the cold and in the middle of a culture shock. As we struggled with the elements, crossing the Downfall one of my mates said: 'If you find pleasure in this sort of thing, well you are definitely not a full shilling. I am never going hiking again in my life.' I think that is what he said, but his words were somehow lost to the cruel wind and water spray which carried bits of sand and pelted your face like thousands of tiny bullets.

And who can blame him, really. But that was him. Maybe in better days things might have been different. But maybe not. Alan Rayner would have loved it, I think.

I could always find excitement just reading about other people's adventures. I remember once I had, a book when I was a kid, about the Canadian Rockies, where some people had this wonderful month among that high area, where they encountered bears, and went swimming in mountain streams, and climbed massive trees. I read the book over and over again, re-living the adventures with the characters of the story.

When I was about fifteen I had a mate whose elder brother went to Iceland for a month at a sort of Outward Bound School. When he returned, tanned and fit looking, he re-lived some of his experiences with me and I was jealous but listened with envy at his tales of glaciers, volcanoes, volcanic rivers and nights full of daylight. I hoped that one day I would get to Iceland, but believing that I never would.

I had read about Icelandic walking holidays for quite a while and had been thinking of suggesting the idea to Alan. But it was expensive, and wondered if I could escape from domestication for two whole weeks. One day passing Alan's desk, I made my suggestion. 'Fancy coming to Iceland for a fortnight, Al?' I asked matter-of-factly. I dropped a leaflet on to his desk, and walked away. It must have been the following day, when he rang me up at home: 'When are we going?' he asked. I could not believe it. I had sold him the idea.

Once, I took a day's holiday to go hiking from Hayfield to Edale, by going down Jacob's Ladder, and Alan Rayner decided to go with me but he had no holidays left. He decided to take a day off sick, and phone in from wherever we could find a telephone. After coming down Jacob's Ladder, eventually, before getting into Edale, you encounter a farm, by the side of which is, or was, a telephone booth.

Alan decided to phone from there. When he got through to work, his boss came on the line, and as Alan was explaining why he was off sick, a queue of farm birds, like a mass exodus, came flapping across the road, geese, hens and ducks, squawking, clucking and quack, quacking. A high pitched crescendo of bird noises that filled the air and the telephone speaker. Alan made his excuses and slammed the phone down before we continued to Edale, laughing all the way.

But now we were going to Iceland for a full two weeks.

Iceland, that place I'd dreamed about, that jagged edged island that sits just below the Arctic Circle, with its south east coast just seven hundred or so miles north west of Scotland and its north westerly tip a mere two or three hundred miles from Greenland. Iceland, that place of mystery, land of fire and volcanic uncertainty, where islands are created overnight by volcanic action that also destroys villages and changes the landscape at a mere whim. We began to study our options and chose a two week guided walking holiday by a company that specialised in Icelandic Holidays. Alan and me always said that we would never do any guided walking, but with Iceland we made an exception. Dick Phillips, based in the lake District, was the company we chose, and once we contacted them, they were quick to let us know that this two week trip was only for experienced fell walkers and the fully fit. I couldn't wait and began reading up on Iceland and getting in a few training sessions with Alan, doing some fast walks over steep areas of the Pennines. Alan informed me that his younger brother, Les was also coming.

We were travelling with Icelandair, catching a plane from Glasgow's Abbotsinch Airport, where we would meet other member of the group. We were told that we were to pick up food parcels that would be waiting for us at the airport, and make sure they got on to the plane. The excitement built up over the weeks, and I began to wonder if I was up to it all.

The plan was to fly to the airport at Keflavik, which was also a military base, then be taken by bus to Reykjavik, where we were to stay for two nights in a youth hostel, by which time other people were to join us and we would meet our guide who would then take us to his home, which was also a hostel, to begin the first day of walking from there. It was summer, so there would be no dark nights at all during our stay, and we would walk every day, to sleep in huts along the

42

route. Every day, we were told, would be different, as the terrain would change from icy slopes to volcanic mountains to wide gushing rivers and whatever else. The prospect looked exciting and inviting, and I could not wait.

Les Rayner lived over a pub at the time, and liked a few pints of Holt's beer as did big brother Alan. What we did not know was that you could not get strong beer in Iceland at that time and the only other alcohol could only be bought at licensed restaurants or at the State Liquor Shops. I think that if Les had known this at the time he would not have gone. Les had not done much hill walking, but he was into diving into underground lakes for fun. I suppose it's whatever turns you on. I met Les for the first time at the train Station in Manchester, from where we would make our way to Scotland. I knew, that whatever else happened, we would have a laugh in Iceland.

Alan Rayner gave me an enormous rucksack, which was necessary to carry the clothing and provisions for our time on the hills, but the prospect of lugging that great weight about for eleven days or so, filled me with dread. It was bad enough carrying it to the station in Manchester. But we laughed all the way to Glasgow, wondering what the other people would be like.

We had to get a bus from the station to the airport and at the Icelandair desk we met some of our new travelling companions. One of them, a fair haired lad with a cheeky grin, was from Blackpool. Then a man and wife team dressed in black thermals were obvious candidates for a fortnight in Iceland, looking as they were ready to whip up the north face of somewhere or other. We all introduced ourselves and chatted excitedly about the forthcoming two weeks.

'Have you done much fell walking?' I asked the male half of the man and wife team, which was a stupid question, considering the way they were dressed.

'Not really,' said he, 'I run most of it.'

It turned out he was a fell runner, and after much chatting, and without an ounce of boasting, he let it slip that he was one of the top three fell runners in the country. Bloody hell, I thought. I'm never going to keep up with these people. Then he let it be known that his wife was the women's fell running world champion. My heart sank and I began to think that Les and I were heading for a hard time over the next two weeks. 'Brilliant,' I said, smiling falsely, trying to hide the fact that I was about to be shown up pretty badly, when the going would get tough.

We were informed that the food parcels were already on the plane, then eventually we too climbed aboard. As we were walking to the plane, a stewardess stopped me and Alan and said something about a cock up with the seating arrangements. As my heart began to sink, the stewardess explained that two of the party would not be able to sit with the others, and would we mind if it was us, bearing in mind that the two seats would be first class, not second class where the others would sit.

'Not at all,' we replied, as one.

Alan and I sat forward of the others then the steward pulled a curtain across the passageway to separate us from the peasants. We were then informed that being in the first class, we were entitled to as many free drinks as we wanted, and suggested that we'd better make the most of it because we would get none in Iceland. Landing at Keflavik, Alan and I were probably the happiest and most glassy eyed passengers around, and noticed that other passengers were piling loads of booze on to shopping trolleys at the duty free shop, to take into the country. A weird arrangement, as if they were trying to tell us something.

We were now in Iceland, and Reykjavik looked gloomy under heavy grey clouds that hung low, threatening much rain. We found our way to the youth hostel, where we booked in and loaded those heavy rucksacks into our rooms. Alan and I were together on the second floor of a room full of bunk beds. The photographs I had seen of Reykjavik, with views from the sea, made it out to be a toy town sort of image, with different coloured buildings, almost a fairyland place. I was surprised to find brick buildings, with gardens, not the sort I would have expected on such unstable ground.

We then went out to explore the town, heading first for the harbour, where the fishing industry is everywhere and provides the country with its main source of income. The smell in places was overpowering, and large trucks ferried millions of fish carcasses everywhere.

I can't remember where we ate that first night, but I can remember Les suggesting that we all get out for a few pints. 'You've no chance,' said Dave, from Blackpool,' they don't sell beer.'

If looks could kill. Les looked at the Blackpool lad as if he was stupid.

'Don't even think of such a thing,' said he. 'I'll find a pub.'

Outside, rain was turning to snow that hit the pavements only to be melted immediately by the warm surface, heated by the underground pipes filled with flowing hot water from the geothermal springs. We pulled our anorak hoods over our heads and made for the town centre as the snow intensified into a blizzard. If it had not been for those hot underground pipes I think that Reykjavik would have disappeared under the whiteness.

'You won't find a pub,' said Dave.

Les swore loudly, then said: 'I'll ask somebody.'

The streets were deserted, with nobody to ask and the heavy sky unloaded much frozen water on to us. Suddenly, from a house a smartly dressed man ran to his car, on which a white carpet was building up.

'Hey, mate, where's the nearest pub?' called Les.

'English?' asked the man, pausing at his car, and obviously not wanting to linger in the snow.

'Yes,' replied Les, 'and dying for a pint.'

'Of beer?' asked the man. The key was in the car door.

Les nodded, his tongue hanging out. His expression said; of course beer, stupid.

'No beer in Reykjavik,' said the man, getting into his car quickly to escape the snow and Les's obscene reply.

'No beer in Reykjavik?' said Les slowly. He looked at us pleadingly and I thought that he was going to cry.

Dave said that he was going his own way and did not want a pint anyway. We carried on deeper into the Reykjavik night, searching for the Holy Grail, a lost cause, thought I. Dave disappeared into the snow instantly.

Eventually, a man staggered across the road, either much the worse for drink or suffering a convulsion. 'He's had booze,' shouted Les, elated. 'Follow him.'

The man swayed and turned towards us. 'Where's the pub?' asked Les, smiling, forming an immediate affinity with the drunk.

The man, some six and a half feet high, wide and thick, and carrying arms like Bluto, shouted something in Icelandic, which we reckoned was hostile to our request, mainly because he was shaking his fists and growling like a monster - a drunken monster.

'I only want a pint,' said Les, 'It's worse than Eccles, here, for trouble.'

Diplomatically, we ran away from the threatening giant, who was closing in like a tank, and turned a corner. Some young people were going into a building from where music trailed out through the opened door.

'That looks interesting,' I said. 'Come on.'

Inside the pub-like building, people sat at tables that where laden with pint-like pots full of honey coloured frothy liquid, and on a small stage, two bearded men played guitars. It had the atmosphere of a folk club and probably was.

'Holt's bitter,' said Les, sighing deeply. 'Who said there's no beer in Reykjavik?'

We sat down at an empty table and I went to the bar where a middle aged barmaid smiled at my request for three pints. 'Three beers', she said, 'and do you want any alcohol in them?'

What on earth was she talking about. I assumed it was the Icelandic sense of humour. Of course I wanted alcohol in them. I nodded meekly, and the woman filled three pots full of beer. Then she got a bottle of something and from it poured out a small measure into what looked like a schnapps glass. From the glass the stuff went into one of the pints. She did the same with the other two pots.

Not at all used to the money system I was still trying to work out what I had paid for the drinks as I returned to the table. It had seemed a lot of kroner. I tried to remember what one kroner was worth.

Les tipped half his beer down his mouth then said: 'That was disgusting, 'which was a true fact that I realised upon tasting my beer. But it was better than nothing and we supped the stuff quickly, so the bad taste would not be noticed. When Alan went to the bar for a refill, we heard him shout: 'How much?' Alan knew the value of the kroner.

'What a rip off,' he said, bringing the beer back to the table. It worked out about two pound fifty a pint, and that was 1984. We finished up drinking pints of wine which was not much more expensive and a lot more potent. Thankfully, the Icelandic laws regarding alcohol have relaxed now, and visitors can get beer and lager in Iceland. It's still expensive but it's the proper stuff and not that rubbish that they gave us. Well, sold us, and extortionately.

That night was my first in Iceland, a strange experience. I was on a top bunk with my head inches from a curtain-less window which let in the never ending daylight. I struggled to get to sleep, and every time I did, Alan, below me, would snore and wake me and a few Icelanders who occupied the other bunks. When I did get to sleep, the sound of many feet clattering on the pavement below disturbed my slumbers and I looked down to the street to see people going to work. I think Alan's snoring had woken up half of Reykjavik, so they had all got up and gone out to work. It was about four o'clock in the morning and Alan slept through it all. It looked like midday in an English summer. Crazy place, Iceland.

The next day, the others came, having flown in from London. A real mixture, including a microbiologist, a doctor, a clinical psychologist, a bloke who ran a formal dress hire company and others. They all looked rather fit and I felt terrible after that sleepless night.

That night, Alan, Les and myself, went to a football match and watched Iceland play Denmark at the Reykjavik sports stadium. Before the big match Iceland's Ladies football team played Iceland's Old Boys, a cracking match. We shouted for the ladies, obviously, who were driven round the running track which surrounded the football pitch, in Rolls Royce cars, before the game. After the game, as we walked to a bus stop, a huge jet of water and steam shot up from the curb, frightening the life out of us. It was a safety valve from the geothermal waters, letting loose its load under pressure.

The next morning, we met our host and guide, Paul, who looked as unfit as Les but fatter. We then had to get a bus to somewhere called Hvolsvollur from where we would be taken to his open aspect des res with rooftop garden and uninterrupted views of a glacier, by a four wheeled drive bus. His home was in Fljotsdalur. The true Iceland opened up before us as we were ferried through an enormous valley that was surrounded by a pillow of snow. We slept that night in a bunker-like dormitory with grass growing wild as a roof.

Paul explained that he hoped that we were all fit and prepared for the coming days, because there would be no going back. He said that we would be walking in all kinds of conditions every day from about ten to five by which time we should reach our intended sleeping accommodation, the huts. The huts, he said, would vary, from the very basic cave-like opening with doors, to the more sophisticated and some would have heating by means of geothermally heated radiators. Paul said that a previous group had to give up after the first day because none of them were fit and they hadn't prepared properly. I began to have doubts about my fitness. Paul said that we looked a fit group, not like the previous one. I hoped he was right.

As we set off along the valley, I did mention to the fell runners that I would find it hard keeping up with them. They reassured me that I'd be all right, and just to go at my own pace. 'It's not a race,' said one of them.

The first few miles were on the flat, along a path to the centre of the valley, and the pace was fast. I've always been quite good on flat conditions; it's when the going gets steep that I struggle, so I was keeping up with the leading group very well. 'I think you've been kidding us,' said a fell runner. 'You are as fit as anybody here.' They would not say that later when the path got steeper.

The rain clouds of the previous day had gone completely and the sky above the valley was a pastel blue as we walked briskly along the path. Spirits were high and all looked forward to the coming days and nights. Sheep grazed on the lower levels, but these were soon left behind as we climbed higher. Much later, a strange looking hill-top loomed before us, which Paul said was near our first hut. This was much easier than I had thought, especially as the sky had got bluer and the day got warmer. Not at all what I'd expected in Iceland. The strange hill-top did not get nearer as we approached it. The hill then seemed to move further away as I got more tired, I imagined the land got steeper. Someone was moving that hill, probably that barmaid with the dodgy beer.

Eventually we were at the hut, the Einhyrningur Hut, surprisingly a two storey affair with doors, windows and corrugated metal walls, a pitched roof, and looking out of place in that flat waste land. The weird hill overlooked the hut like a guardian. It was about five o'clock in the evening and I did not feel too bad, but I welcomed the rest. With some of the others, I sat down on the grassy ground and properly surveyed the surroundings. The green valley stretched a mile or so wide, with a peat bog type of hilly landscape - reminding me of Kinder - to one side and a snow covered, mountainous moonscape to the other. The crazy hill looked like an alien nearby, with an almost phallic top pointing upwards towards the blue sky. Offloading my heavy rucksack, I stretched out on the flat ground and considered sunbathing. Les sat besides me with similar intentions.

'This is the life,' said Les, his eyes shut to the blueness above. 'Not a hard start, was it?'

'Right, everybody in the hut to offload, then you can climb that hill while I make dinner.' Paul's voice interrupted my peace, and I could not quite muster the enthusiasm being shown by the others. But for purely social reasons, I followed the crowd to dump my rucksack in the hut and then joined them outside again for the start of our hill climb. The fell runners were half way up before I had began to think about it and were half way down again when I was out of breath on the way up. But at the top, the view was stunning, looking out across vast snow covered areas.

That night we were introduced to two subjects which were to be part of our lives for the remainder of our time in the wilderness; skyr and the shit shovel.

Firstly, skyr, a mildly sour, rich type of curd, which was to become the main ingredient of our diet for the next few days and was to be cunningly mixed with other lifeboat rations such as dried food, it added a rare much needed blandness to everything we ate.

Secondly, the shit shovel. This implement was the main accessory to every hut. No self respecting Reykjavik estate agent would ever advertise a mountain hut without offering this crucial tool as part of the deal. The shit shovel usually lived over or- near to the front door. But this was not for decorative purposes. The shit shovel's thing in life was to accompany people to a mountain latrine of their choice, be it an icy waste, a snowy mountain top, or an open-aspected spot by the side of a fast flowing volcanic river. It was the most used piece of equipment and its sharp pointed blade was designed to dig into any frozen ground of your choice. It was an environmentally friendly shovel, designed to tell no tales of the many little hidden toilets that litter the Icelandic wastes.

One hut though, towards the middle of the trip, came with a detached khazi. This posh number had a little outbuilding nearby, built over a deep snowy slope. Inside, a plank with two holes, side by side, straddled over the slope, down which one's faeces dropped into its frozen depth. The rumour was that once full, the hut would be moved slightly sideways. This toilet was built on an exposed and windy hillside allowing the icy wind to blow under the hut and gather momentum as it whistled through the holes over which bare bottoms loomed. Needless to say, nobody ever lingered long on this toilet. Not the sort of place to take the Daily Mirror or Reykjavik Times for twenty minutes.

Sometimes the evening meals began with soup made from powdered ingredients which were boiled with water that sometimes had to be made by melting snow. The main course would have skyr added to whatever else could be created from Paul's kitchen of dried surprises. However towards the end of the trip, the food began to become delicious. Ships biscuits also became part of our diet. I have to say that food was not the main turn-on of the trip.

Everywhere we went was unpronounceable, Hvolsvollur, Fljottsdalur, Einhyrninger, Krokur, Laufafell, Hrafntinusker, Landmannalauger, Jokulgilskvisl, Alftavatn and so on. The list was lengthy and mind boggling. We crossed a fast flowing river that tried to kill us but it was easier to cross than pronounce.

It was obvious after that first day that the others on the trip were all either reasonably fit or very fit. Going up that hill while Paul made dinner reminded me of the hill we all had to run up at the Outward Bound School at eighteen, a sort of test to see how fit we were. I wondered if that was the reason Paul suggested it, to see how fit we were, after a day's walking.

The next day, the sky was cloudy and dull looking, and we set off early into the unknown, following Paul as usual. It would become apparent over the next few days that Paul was very fit in spite of his size and a superb mountaineer as well. Paul lived in the Lake District during winter but spent summers in Iceland as a guide. He had been, as we found out later, a squash champion. As I said, a very fit man, and good company.

On this second day, the terrain was changing appearance already. Wide precipitous cracks appeared in the ground, through which raging white water cascaded down, and suddenly our walking was over a carpet of continuous snow. Then the weather became duller and threatened to rain as we approached a wide shallow river of clear fast flowing water. Paul remarked that rivers in Iceland were meant to be waded through and that this one was no exception. In fact wading rivers would become a feature of our Icelandic days from now on, and on one occasion, because we were so used to wading rivers, we actually waded one that had a bridge nearby.

The walking was getting harder as the land began to undulate, and small hills and mountains became the backdrop to everything. By the time the second hut came into sight, I was getting tired and looked forward to getting my big rucksack off my back where it felt that it was becoming part of me. This second hut was only a single storey affair, of metal cladded walls and a flat roof, with a lovely view of snow capped hills behind it. I dropped my rucksack and some of us went to explore the area locally while Paul acted as chef. Large rivers poured through valleys carved in the volcanic ground and the sky had turned to white above. Iceland was just as I had expected it to be and long dead volcanoes resided everywhere, between which the fast flowing waters of streams and rivers wove in irregular patterns.

We were steadily getting to know the others and they were getting to know us. They would soon get to know snoring from hell, Eccles style.

It was probably on the second night that one of the group, Gerald, from London, would become our very best friend. Gerald, who ran a formal dress hire business, had brought with him a selection of liqueurs; in fact his rucksack seemed to be full of them. When he asked did we want a drink, we wondered what he was talking about, but our faces lit up when he produced a bottle of liqueur. It might have been creme-de-menthe or something like that, but whatever it was, it was wonderfully received in that desolate hut, especially by Alan, Les and myself. We later found excellent use for Gerald's liqueurs by mixing them with some of the more tasteless of Paul's dried foods, which was all of them. Gerald seemed to have the biggest rucksack, and we reckoned it was because it was full of these drinks. Gerald also had brought a pair of slippers which he would wear at night in the huts. If he came again, said Gerald, he would stop in a hotel.

The events in Iceland will from now on not be in chronological order, mainly because I can't remember in what order they occurred, and I couldn't pronounce them if I could, but I will try to highlight the amusing incidents that happened.

Wading through fast flowing rivers became a daily occurrence from day two, and we endured every type of weather possible, from heavy rain, gale force winds, snow and fog. The huts were from the very basic to the very good, in fact one of them had people running it, who cooked our meals.

One night, in a two storey hut, Les, Alan, a female member and myself were on the ground floor of a hut with the others asleep above, when Les started to snore. The woman sharing the ground floor with us gave up in the end and climbed up the ladder to join the others upstairs, leaving Alan and myself to endure the din. The noise eventually became unbearable and the upstairs lot banged on the floor and shouted. The hills must have been alive with the sound of snoring and shouting. We could stand it no more, so Alan began to shake his brother violently, which had no effect. So Alan started to kick Les, which resulted in some loud moans mixed in with the snoring, but he did not wake up. The shouting from the upstairs noise abatement society grew louder and more distraught. Finally, nothing else having worked, Alan and I picked up the sleeping bag with Les in it, and then dropped it from a height of about two feet from the ground. Les slept through it all, so not wanting to injure Les, we left him snoring for what remained of the night. In the morning, we were all tired and red eyed and Les complained of having had a terrible night's sleep.

The hut which I mentioned had the detached toilet block, also had a most glorious view from a nearby hill. We took photographs at midnight from this hill with the sun peeping from behind the horizon, an amazing sight.

I remember once, after a very tiring day, I collapsed by the door of our hut for the night, with my rucksack still attached. The relief of reaching that hut was overpowering and I just sat there propped up against the great weight on my back, collecting my breath and taking in the view of wall to wall glaciers. As Paul began to prepare the evening meal, the fell runners went fell running, and I watched in amazement as the pair ran across the valley to scamper up a mountain like a pair of young goats, then to disappear in the distance. Half an hour later they returned and the meal was prepared. I think I was fast asleep at the time.

The scenery, changing every day, gave us everything that Iceland had to offer, from pools of boiling red mud that spit up great dollops of steaming sludge, resembling some of the curries I had made at home, to enormous frozen lakes, great fields of lava, perfectly formed extinct volcanoes, glacial rivers and endless snow topped mountains.

Sometimes the walking was easy but sometimes very hard, especially when over deep snow or hard ice, and once we had to cross a frozen lake to get to our hut. The lake, said Paul, was very deep and the ice on the top was beginning to melt, due to the high summer temperature. Our feet sank in the snow and melting ice, making it very hard work to get across. Eventually our feet were sinking a foot or so under the top surface and the hut on the other side seemed an eternity away. Getting to that hut was probably the greatest relief of the trip.

Another time, we used our foam sleeping rolls as sledges to slide down a snowy slope, a wonderful feeling in the middle of nowhere, in a blizzard and thick fog. Looking at the photographs, now, it is hard to believe that we had such good fun in those terrible conditions. It was a good job we had Paul with us to know where we were.

One of the huts was overlooked by a very steep, snow covered hillside, and with some time to spare, an unusual event, I suggested we tried sliding down the slope, again using our foam rolls as sledges. The hard part was getting to the top of the hill. After a hesitant start, one of us made a successful but hair raising slide down the hill to crash land in a pile of snow. Then we all clambered up to slide down again. It was then that imagination took over and the competitive side of our natures crept in. It started with getting marks for artistic merit but soon developed into other things, such as the men's double with Les Rayner clinging for dear life to his brother who rode at the front on the foam roll. I think they parted company half way down and finished up twenty feet from each other after tumbling down in different directions. The mixed doubles had the fell runners crashing downwards and I think the men's treble was a complete disaster right from the start. This went on for an hour or two, a very dangerous but enjoyable way to spend an afternoon in Iceland.

Every day brought different but wonderful scenery, and I think each new day was just a bit better than the day before. As I look back I think it was that diversity of scenery that made the whole trip so interesting and without any boredom creeping in.   -

Now I have always considered myself a bit outgoing and the sort who makes myself known to everybody, warts and all, within hours of meeting them. The same could probably be said of my friends from Eccles too. I must have come on too strong with one of the others, who suggested that I was in hysteria, that first time we all met in the hostel in Reykjavik, when I was joking and laughing with Alan. Let me tell you that after a few days out in the wilderness, some of the others began to change their personalities, while I was still the same old me. I recited some of my silly poems one night, which made the others giggle, something I don't think could have happened that first night. One of the group seemed to change personality completely and became a sort of wild man, not shaving and wanting to light fires everywhere we went.

Only once did we see any other people on the hills, and that was towards the end of our time in the wilderness. There was a large group of walkers some distance away, appearing like small dots hardly moving over the rounded top of a snow covered mountain. Jokes became the norm and from people who initially were the quiet ones. The main topic of our jokes were the shit shovel, the food, the huts and each one of us. Probably in that order.

The day before the last, of our time on the hills, we were going over a lava field, a wide valley full of irregular shaped rocks with sharp edges, where walking was difficult, and time had to be taken to manoeuvre one's feet over pumice. Suddenly I slipped and as I tried to reach one of my feet on to a stable rock, I felt the most excruciating pain in my knee which coincided with a sickening click that seemed as loud as Les' snoring. I collapsed in a heap clutching my damaged knee and the hills were alive with the sound of my swearing. My knee swelled to the size of a large orange, inflated by a cushion of fluid. But help was at hand by one of the group, a doctor. One thing about being in Iceland, he had no trouble making an ice pack, which cooled the hotness in my knee and reduced the pain somewhat. But from then on my walking was severely restricted and I missed out on some wonderful sights, although Alan took photographs on the walks that I missed and later gave me the copies when we returned to England. My greatest regret is missing the awesome sight of the waterfall at Ofaerufoss although, as I said, I have got the pictures of it from Alan's films.

One of the huts was at a place called Landmannalauger, a magnificent two storey desirable residence that came with resident hosts and hot running water in the form of large pools, geothermically heated just some hundred metres from the huts. Approaching that hut was like approaching the Hilton. It was here that the laugh was on me. As we approached this wonderful sight from our time in the waste lands, we couldn't believe that we would be staying in such a plush building. The hut was the largest yet and two toned, with a green roof and dark wooded walls. It even had a pathway to it, lined by rocks and it stood out on the flat dark ground with a snowy hill beyond. As we were but metres away, Paul said something about hoping that the wardens were at home. They were. As we turned the corner of the hut, two girls were sunbathing on towels under the bright sun that burned down from a cloudless blue sky. I thought for a moment that we were in Spain or that the skyr had turned my brain, but the snow opposite spoilt that illusion. The girls wore only bikini bottoms apart from maybe some sun oil, and we had disturbed their siesta. The sight was almost surreal to me. Us, unshaven (the men) not having met anybody for over a week, hardly washed and knackered from the walk, having slept on straw, been acquainted with the shit shovel for a week, and now in the giggly, talking silly stage, were faced with two firm young bodies under an Icelandic sun. Was it all an illusion, the effect of eating dried foods for a week, wading through countless rivers and having every attempt at sleep disturbed by snoring that resembled a machine gun being fired?

The illusions moved. 'Ah, the English people, we've been expecting you.' One of the illusions got up to welcome us. I just couldn't picture her with a shit shovel. One of our group, the most unshaven, looking like Bigfoot on a bad day, gazed at those firm breasts obsessively. Then his camera appeared from nowhere and he took on the roll of a Daily Sport photographer. 'I bet you would like a hot drink?' said the girl, disregarding Bigfoot, which was probably the biggest understatement of all time.

I collapsed as usual, on the hard ground, leaning on the rucksack that had now become part of me as our group were in discussion with the Icelandic girls. Then one of the girls said. 'Alan, would you help?' she was looking down at me. The others gazed in my direction. 'We need water,' said the girl. The others nodded. 'It your turn,' added one of our group.

'At the end of the path is a small waterfall,' said the Icelandic girl, passing me a bucket. She pointed to some far distant place. It was the sort of place the fell runners would normally have run to, after a day's trudging.

'Okay,' I said, untangling myself from the rucksack and I got to my feet, smiling with false enthusiasm.

'Just follow the small path,' said the girl, as I grabbed the bucket.

'Hurry up,' said someone, 'I'm thirsty.

I forced my tired legs into a jog, as if it came natural to me, and the others cheered. The waterfall seemed a long way away, but I reached it eventually and filled the bucket to the brim. Voices from afar filled the air. 'Hurry up. We're thirsty. Come on, Butty. Full to the brim. The bucket was full, so I turned for the homeward straight, mindful not to spill too much. They were cheering. Why were they cheering? And they were waving and clapping. It was no big deal. I was tempted to move faster but already the bucket was wobbling and an inch of water had been lost. It was heavy so I swapped arms.

'We'll never get that cup of tea'. But then I was back, smiling; the one who had been for water. Everybody clapped like I was a hero. I felt as if I was blushing. Alan Rayner was laughing hysterically.

'You've spilt most of it,' moaned someone. 'You'll have to go back,' said another. But they were giggling, and I sensed that all was not as it should be.

'It does not matter,' said a topless Icelandic girl,' we can fill it up at the tap.'

The hills were alive with the sound of much laughter that must have been heard in Reykjavik. There was a tap, a bloody tap, and right there fixed to the wall of the hut. And I had been on an extracurricular hike to get water. But they were happy. And if they were happy, then I was happy.

Later, after the tea, and after stashing away our belongings, we were told of the geothermal pools nearby, where residents of Reykjavik come to bathe regularly. I don't think that we had washed properly, not an all over wash, for many days and the thought of jumping into hot water seemed luxury.

It was agreed that the two women went first, then when they had dried, dressed and returned, all the men headed for the pools, which seemed to be rivers from which steam rose into the air. We all stripped off and leaving clothes and towels by the poolside, we all climbed into the water. It was exhilarating with the hot water, some areas hotter than others, doing wonderful things to my aching muscles and washing away all the dried sweat and smell. We stayed in the water for ages and swam where it was deep enough to do so. Sometimes the water was too hot and we had to move to cooler parts. The whole thing now seemed worth while. A bar selling Holt's bitter, when we got back to the hut, would have really been seen as the icing on the cake, but that was not to be.

Eventually most of us reluctantly climbed out of the hot water, dried ourselves, dressed and made our way across the narrow timber pathway that had been laid across the dark volcanic ground between the hot pools and the hut. Three remained in the water.

Then there were two in the water, Les and another guy, and someone was coming across that timber path, dressed but carrying clothes, the clothes belonging to the two left in the pool. People dashed back to the hut to get cameras, as voices from the poolside cursed and carried on. "Hey you bastards, where's our clothes?"

Cameras waited, primed, ready. Good, I thought. It was like getting my own back after the bucket episode. The flat bed of the valley was mottled green over stony volcanic ground and overhead the sky was a deep blue with signs of wispy clouds in the distance. The narrow timber pathway disappeared into a vanishing point at the foot of some low, green topped hills overlooking the pools. Then the pink bodies appeared from that vanishing point, running precariously across the timbers towards us. Much shouting and cheering accompanied the naked runners. I cheered also. Now it was somebody else's turn. The pink bodies neared, not amused, but we all were, as were our hostesses, who must have seen it all before. That was definitely the best hut of the trip.

On the very last day in the wilderness, we were picked up by a four wheel drive bus and taken back to the hostel in Reykjavik where we spent our last night in Iceland. I remember a sadness mixed with an anti-climactic atmosphere amongst us as we climbed aboard that four wheel drive bus with the high chassis. The photograph of us waiting to board the bus, I think, pictures the reflective mood of the group. On the way back to Reykjavik we stopped to have a look at a sort of heritage museum which consisted of some huts that blended into the hillside with their grassed over roofs. As we were coming out of the heritage museum, a bus pulled up and twenty or so elderly German geologists were unloaded on to the volcanic ground. They then walked solemnly into the museum and I wondered if they had had as good a time as we had. Probably not. I bet that they had not joked about a shit shovel or lived on a diet of cardboard, or boiled snow to get water.

The last evening in Reykjavik was very anti-climactic, and we went to a cafe in the centre for a meal. The joking was stilted, probably because the jokes were old now and well worn. The next day, at the airport, the Icelandair aeroplane was as grey as the sky. Greyness prevailed as we boarded, but we were going home to our families, proper beds which were miles from Les' snoring, food that would taste of food, and beer, proper beer of alcoholic content.

We did intend to get together again, back in Britain, on a regular basis but after the first few meetings, it fizzled out. Alan and myself did organise a meeting in Hayfield, during which we stayed overnight in the Sportsman pub. I led a hike over Kinder in Icelandic conditions. Paul and his wife had cycled down from the Lake District. He actually did the hike wearing shorts. Other hikers could not believe it in such bad weather. It was a good turn out but only about two thirds of the party turned up. Our pal, Peter Glyn, came also and we shared a room during which I tried to pee in Peter's wardrobe after a heavy night's drinking.

Alan and myself did say that we would return to Iceland and maybe one day we will, especially now that one can get a decent drink in the place, even if it is at an extortionate cost. We would probably have take to out a mortgage to pay for a proper Icelandic booze up. It is certainly the sort of place one does not forget, and I would recommend it to anybody who is serious about walking and seeing fabulous sights.

Touring clubs now offer seeing Iceland by horse, jeep or even by bicycle if you are crazy enough for that over the bumpy roads and paths. It was not so long ago that the horse was the only form of transport and even now travelling by horse is the best way to get to some of the way out places. If you are a birdwatcher, Iceland is your paradise, with many species making up the bird population, both indigenous and migratory. But to me, it's the scenery that is Iceland, the places of natural beauty which make up its interior. I only saw a small part of this and was amazed by how the scenery changed by the day. If you go, you will see magnificent waterfalls, belts of volcanic craters, eruptions of steam and hot springs. You will see the melted water from glaciers form fast flowing rivers that will not be there the next day, and you may feel the ground under your feet move with volcanic action. Around the coast you will see rugged cliffs and rocks in bizarre shapes, and from the northern coast you will see icebergs floating past.

Iceland is the land of the sagas which were written in the thirteenth century and are legends of the lives of various families, mostly outlaws, who existed some few hundred years before they were written. The average saga is of rape, pillage and bloodshed - typical Icelandic family soaps. Most Icelanders are familiar with the characters - a sort of thirteenth century Coronation Street with gore.

An important day of modern Iceland was 1st of March, 1989 when the ban on strong beer was lifted and great crowds celebrated in very cold conditions. I think everybody got absolutely rat-legged and wrecked Reykjavik, giving the government second thoughts on lifting the ban. Les Rayner would have enjoyed that day in Reykjavik.

A local Icelandic delicacy is pickled ram's testicles. Another delight is shark that has been buried underground for a few months. This dish is washed down with a local Icelandic spirit. Almost every part of a sheep is considered as food; the most notorious is the sheep's head, burned to remove the wool, and then boiled. It is served with turnips. It would have to taste better than it looks. At the end of our trip I think I would have eaten any of these things.

6   MALLORCA

Mallorca, largest of the Balearic Islands, famous for scorching sun, blue skies, sangria, and sandy beaches looking out to the Mediterranean Sea. Little is said of the stunning sights: shear cliffs and superb walks up steep mountains.

The first time I went to Mallorca, was with Sylvia, on a last minute booking affair, so we did not know where we were staying. At Palma Airport, the Spanish holiday rep turned up drunk then left without us, which resulted in us spending the night at the airport, until the following morning when we could telephone for help and be told the name of the hotel we were staying in. After a sleepless night we got a taxi to an old Spanish hotel in Palma Nova, where we stayed for the rest of the fortnight. Not a good start to the holiday, but we did have a good time, during which time we saw the worst of Magaluf which was only a stones throw away. It was the early eighties in years and the late eighties in temperature. Not a place, one would think, as a possible hiking venue.

But not long after that holiday, I saw an article in a newspaper which described a cliff walk to the west of Mallorca, and a photograph showed a rugged cliff edge with a narrow path overlooking a shear drop into the Mediterranean Sea below. Another photograph showed a lush valley looking like some lost world from which dinosaurs might charge out of. This was not the Mallorca I had been to. The article had me intrigued and made the place out to be some walkers haven, describing wonderful scenery and steep drops into blue sea. The place describe was Sa Colobra, a small village which one could walk to along this cliff edge, then catch a boat back to a place called Puerto Soller, a holiday resort. The article mentioned that one would not meet many people there. Not like the beach at Magaluf.

The article did mention that the whole of that area was a walker's dream, especially inland, where it described high, rugged mountains. I was curious and not long after, another article appeared in a newspaper describing another walk, a steep climb up a mountain in Mallorca. I collected the two articles and began to make enquiries into going to Mallorca to spend a full week walking, with the odd social drinking evening of course. At the time there were not many books on walking in Mallorca, but I did manage to get a recently published book, Walking in Mallorca, by June Parker, a handy sized book describing many of Mallorca's best walks in reasonable detail. My interest was growing and then I phoned up McCarta Ltd of London, who sent me a grid of all the Spanish Military Maps, the only ones available then, of the walking and climbing areas of Spain and its Islands. I ordered the ones I considered necessary for my intended walking holiday in Mallorca. The maps at 1:50,000 scale looked interesting and showed pathways over the mountains, but were not to the standard of our Ordnance Survey maps. But the maps showed a Mallorca as I never envisaged, with masses of open spaces, high mountains and rugged coastlines. The towns and villages were few and far between. Also the maps were old, therefore changes must surely have been made since their original survey. After a few weeks, I had decided on which walks I would attempt and had typed out routes and map co-ordinates with little line diagrams showing place names.

I decided that Puerto Soller would be the place to stay, mainly because it was near enough to the main walking area. It was a holiday resort therefore would contain bars, and that various forms of transport were easily accessible from there, train, buses and taxis.

But who would come with me? Alan Rayner was already committed that year with his walking holiday and I did consider going to Mallorca alone but not for long.

A long standing mate of mine, Frank, who lived just around the corner, had recently been accompanying me on some small hikes around Derbyshire and was just about getting into the walking scene. Frank was, as I soon found out, a natural map reader and route finder by using the sun to detect where north was. He had not had any training on map reading but it all came natural to him and he was very rarely, if at all, wrong. He was a tool maker, or precision engineer, as he liked to call it, by trade, and applied his trade's attention to detail to everything else he did, which now included map reading. But it was, and is, Frank's dry sense of humour that makes him a perfect walking companion, and a companion in general. Our nights out were always hilarious as were our family get together. Frank, I knew would have been perfect for a week in Mallorca but the least person I expected to come with me. When I half heartedly mentioned Mallorca to him I was surprised at his enthusiasm and even more surprised when he agreed to come with me. He showed great interest in the maps and was amazed at the amount of open space and mountainous area on the holiday island.

We picked a small hotel in Puerto Soller, right on the front facing the sea and booked it as a package, being picked up at Palma airport by coach. I couldn't wait. Also coming with us was Paul who was at the time engaged to my youngest daughter, Karen.

I love the build up to the walking holidays, with all the planning and this was no exception and I spent ages going over all the walks that were planned. I went into a sort of a training regime with Frank, mainly going to Derbyshire, around the Derwent area, just off the Snake Road next to Ladybower Reservoir. We would park up on the visitor's car park next to Derwent Reservoir and then walk briskly by various paths along the top, passing Lost Lad, Cakes of Bread and on to one of the paths down again, then back to the car park. In good weather these walks offer great views down to the reservoirs but can be very muddy in wet weather, although these days sections of the main path have been flagged with large cut stones. As the weeks went by, we speeded up and Frank's cigarette smoking lessened a little which much improved his fitness. Also I had started jogging on the hills to improve my fitness.

It was an afternoon flight and Manchester Airport was, as usual, heaving. Paul and myself were dressed as if we were going hiking somewhere but Frank wore a blazer, shirt and tie, and a pair of shades. He looked like James Bond with a rucksack. James Bond had had a little drink to steady his nerves for the flight and was in a chatty mood. Some elderly women holiday makers, in the queue behind us, asked Frank if we were mountaineers, to which he replied that we were professional mountaineers and geologists. The bullshit was starting early. I kept out of the conversation and Paul shook his head. I knew that this was going to be a good trip, which is what it turned out to be.

The coach trip from Palma Airport started off on the flat but eventually we began to climb higher as we encountered the start of the mountains, a part of Mallorca I had never seen. Then the coach came upon the scary hairpin bends on the mountain road and we were going down again and into Puerto Soller. The town is very picturesque with palm trees around the small sand and shingle beach to the bay, and views of nearby mountains gives it a character all of its own. The family resort has shops, bars and restaurants, mostly facing the enclosed bay. Five kilometres away from Puerto Soller is the inland town of Soller, from where some of the walks begin, and the two towns are connected by an electric tram system. There is a privately run train service linking Soller with Palma.

It was evening and the sky was darkening. Outside the family run hotel, chairs and tables were set out under a canopy, and facing was the bay. We were booked in at half board and hoped the we were not too late for the evening meal. We signed in, handed our passports to the clerk, and dumped our gear in the small, narrow room with a sea view. Three beers were ordered at the bar and consumed immediately before we went into the restaurant and sat at a table with our room number on it.

'Hola,' greeted a waiter, with a courteous nod

'Hola,' returned Frank.

'Would you like a drink?' asked the waiter, hovering.

'Tres cervezas grande,' replied Paul who had been practising.

'Si.'

The man came back with three large beers, and then came the soup at the same time as our glasses were empty.

'Can we have the wine list?' asked Frank.

'Certainly,' nodded the waiter. He looked up at the ceiling, considering all options, then said: 'We have white wine and we have red wine.'

'Ah, quite a choice,' said Frank. 'We'll have the red.'

'A good choice,' said the waiter, tapping his nose with a forefinger before turning on his heels with a knowing and contented smile.

'Class place, this,' I said.

The bottle of red wine came a few minutes before our main meal, which was good timing.

'We must try the white another evening,' said Frank.

'Then we've gone through the wine list,' I said.

'Then we'll start again,' said Frank.

An agreeable idea.

After the average meal and the adequate wine, we sauntered out onto the Puerto Soller promenade to sample the delights of its night life, finding plenty of bars and restaurants to investigate over the coming week. Puerto Soller, we found out, goes suddenly black at night, as if a light switch has been flicked, the reaction of the sun hiding quickly behind a nearby mountain. Frank, in case of a possible emergency, bought a litre bottle of cheap brandy to take back to our room. I had a bottle of whisky, bought at the duty free in Manchester. Emergency rations were therefore accounted for.

Later that night we noticed some English people booking in the hotel. One, a woman, was giving orders to the others, as a prison guard might to a bunch of high security prisoners. 'And we don't want to have a late night if we've got to be up early in the morning, do we? A nice long hike, tomorrow,' she added, half to herself.

The others shook their heads in agreement. Some looked enthusiastic, others smiled falsely. The boss woman glared at us as we ordered tres cervazas grande, just for a night-cap, then stomped towards the stairs with her chest and chin stuck out like a sergeant major

With our beer glasses we sauntered out to the hotel front, under the canopy. Some of the new group were there talking in whispered tones. A scattering of holiday makers walked past under the dense black sky.

'Going walkies, then?' asked Frank of the group.

One turned, nodded. The middle aged woman shook her head. 'I'm having second thoughts already.' The others preferred not to comment.

'We're going hiking tomorrow,' said Frank.

'Do you want to take her with you?' asked the one speaking to us, nodding towards the hotel.

'No thanks,' replied Frank.

The group of hikers smiled glumly and sauntered back into the hotel.

Later, back in our room, Frank took the bed nearest the window, mine was nearest the door, and Paul's was somewhere in between. I opened my bottle of whisky and took a swig before getting in to bed. Frank took his cheap brandy and one of the toothbrush glasses to his bedside. Paul was already asleep, and soundly.

Eventually Frank said goodnight, which I just heard through the bedclothes. 'Goodnight,' I muttered in return, and was aware of the room being plunged into darkness as Frank switched off his bedside lamp. All was quiet but for Paul's heavy breathing. I was relaxed and tired, and soon settled into a sort of daydream, thinking of the proposed walk for the following day. Then the daydream was becoming a proper dream as I lapsed into near subconscious, but my head was filled with mountain-top views. I don't know how long I had been asleep, if at all, when the noise occurred. A creaking sound that interrupted my alfresco visions, then a bang sent the mountain views dashing from my head.

I sat up in the darkness as Frank switched on the light. 'Bloody hell, what's that?' he muttered.

'It was in the room,' I said.

The next thing, Frank was out of bed, investigating, but his investigations did not last long. 'It's my wardrobe door,' he announced, with his hands on the culprit, which had swung open and crashed into the woodwork. Frank closed the door, pushing it firmly into place. But before he managed to get back under the sheets, the door swung open again, with the same creak. Frank swore and closed the door again, pressing it in place before releasing it. The door held fast. 'I'm not a precision engineer for nothing,' he said, getting back into bed. Switching the light off coincided with the door opening again. This time we both got out of bed and attacked the door without success. The damn thing just opened straight away this time.

Frank reached for his brandy, just for inspiration, and had a swig. He was grinning as he replaced the top on the bottle, then he closed the wardrobe door, putting the bottle on the floor hard up against the door. The door strained but did not move. 'Told you I was a precision engineer,' he said triumphantly, getting back into bed.

The door and bottle remained in place then for the night, and I returned to my mountains and glorious views, and then slept soundly and peacefully until I was awoken by Paul moving about the room. It was morning and daylight filled the room from the window behind Frank's bed. Frank then got up and looked through the window that overlooked the promenade and bay. He lit a cigarette, out of habit, and laughed. 'That lot are up early,' he said. 'And she's giving orders again!

I struggled over the brandy bottle, passed Paul's bed, to the window, and looked out. Down below, one woman gave orders, gesticulating with her arms. Others looked bewildered. The woman's voice boomed, probably waking everybody in the hotel, who had decided to lie in: and everybody in Puerto Soller as well. The morning tranquillity of Puerto Soller was shattered as it probably was over the north west of Mallorca. Her who shall be obeyed was being obeyed with no questions asked. Our hangovers felt worse for the noise. The few early morning tourists and the those Mallorcans, maybe on their way to work, looked oddly at the bossy woman, and crossed over the road to avoid getting caught up in the order taking. A bus appeared and those being ordered were ordered on the bus. Were they being taken away to be shot by firing squad? No, they were going hiking, just like us.

The continental breakfast was eaten in silence, whilst three rucksacks, like little dogs waiting to be taken walkies, parked by our chairs. Our day was planned, but we needed some food for our day on the mountains. Minutes later, the people in the local supermarket who were very friendly, made us sandwiches of cheese and ham on bread rolls. We took bottled water to drink. The warmth of the day was already making itself known.

First we had to get to Soller, three miles away, and to get there we had to get on the tram which runs on tracks along the sea front of Puerto Soller. The locals reckon that the tramcars have been imported from San Francisco, and they look the part. The journey to Soller was picturesque, looking out to citrus groves, a sight we were to become accustomed to. The town of Soller is well known throughout the Island as a centre for lemons and oranges which are sold every Saturday on the local market. Soller, said to be the birthplace of Christopher Columbus, nestles in a picturesque setting, in a valley, between high mountains, and was once virtually inaccessible. But not now, thanks to the tram.

In the centre of Soller, a town square is surrounded by cafes and restaurants, a charismatic place to idle away one's time. We commented on the possibility of us staying in Soller one day.

Our first walk on the island of Mallorca was to be started by climbing up what is known locally as the Pilgrim steps from a place called Biniaraix, close to Soller, then over some high level paths, and then back down again into Soller. On the way to the start of the Pilgrim steps, we found a place that sold orange juice squeezed from fresh oranges and served in a tall glass with plenty of ice. Strangely, the weather on our first walk was not what we expected, with plenty of cloud overhead with the mountain tops partly hidden with mist. But it was warm, and that welcoming chilled fresh orange juice was consumed quickly before we made our way to the Pilgrim steps. The steps were in fact a cobbled path that wove its way upwards, seemingly for ever, through fantastic scenery. The higher we got the more of Mallorca we could see. The sides of the steps were lined with stones and beyond the stones, the hillside was cleverly landscaped to look natural. Waterfalls cascaded down through the trees and exotic plants, and once a peacock strutted its stuff just a metre from the path, its highly coloured patterns blending in with the foliage.

Other walkers were coming down the hill and we were not aware of anybody else going up it. Those coming down were very wise because the steepness increased as did the height, and I was sweating profusely, in spite of the lack of sunlight. 'Morning,' I greeted to a couple, through laboured breaths. They were coming down and breathing normally. 'Guten morgan,' greeted both of them, then said something in German. Moments later, a group of people filled the path in front of me. 'Morning,' I managed to utter, breathing deeply. 'Gutten morgan,' said many German voices as I shuffled between the descending crowd. A while later, another couple strode downwards before me. 'Morgan,' said the man, ' then he laughed and said something in German that made him laugh all the more. I nodded. 'Morgan,' I said, smiling. The next time, I beat them to it. 'Gutten morgan,' I greeted the next couple who loomed ahead. The man nodded. Then as he passed me he said to his female companion: 'They're all German here, have you noticed.' Below me I heard Frank greet them. 'Morgan.'

The walk was getting steeper and more picturesque, and I was breathing and sweating heavily as the day got warmer. There is in Mallorca, a conservation group called ICONA which does a marvellous job of looking after the mountain trails amongst other things, and I believe take the credit for the tidiness of the Pilgrim steps and its landscaping.

A lot of Guten morgans were exchanged and the odd 'Gruss Gott.' before we reached the top of the ascent, by which time I was dripping in sweat. Frank was lagging behind, and occasionally he would stop to light a cigarette. Little puffs of smoke could be seen rising like Indian signals through the exotic foliage. Frank had been trying to cut down on his smoking and walking up hills certainly aided this, although when we did get to the top, he told us how many cigarettes he'd had. He said that he was going to grade his walks from now on, by how many cigarettes he smoked during a walk. The steps had been a four cig walk, so it was quite a steep one.

As the ground evened out and the cobbles gave way to parched soil, we stopped to rest.

'God, I'm ....' Frank was about to say.

A flapping of wings made us jump and right at our feet a red beaked drake dropped on the back of a duck and proceeded to mate frantically.

'Exactly,' laughed Frank. 'He's got more energy than me. 'I'll have a cigarette for him.' Frank lit up to celebrate as specks of fine rain came down to cool our faces, a welcomed event of nature. We all had a drink of bottled water, then moved on as the rain got heavier. From there, wonderful views of mountains were everywhere, scenes that could never be observed from below where tourists abound. We moved on, through a farm, then stopped to look at the map as a fine mist suddenly appeared from nowhere, shrouding the higher levels. Fearing that the mist might get worse, we moved on along the path that was marked in places by small blobs of paint, cunningly applied to rocks, but done to appear as natural markings, all done by ICONA (El Instituto National para la Conservacion de la Naturaleza) But sometimes one had to look carefully to find these markings, and often we confused natural markings for them. But the way ahead was reasonably clear and the mist began to clear again, leaving us with the fine views of grey mountains speckled with green shrubs. Looking downwards, rugged, knobbly hills eventually gave way to the lower gently undulating countryside leading to the Med, but Mallorca's coastline was obscured by fine mist. We pressed on, over parched ground with scatterings of limestone rocks and sparse vegetation, eventually making a descent through a wooded area. From the top of the Pilgrim steps, we did not encounter another living being, other than countless butterflies, wild birds and quick moving lizards that scuttled out of sight as we approached. The wooded descent was like a fairyland, and there the trees were marked with tiny spots of paint showing us the way. Eventually, the way down took us out of the trees and on to a rough vehicle track leading to a road, where we got a bus back to Soller, some well chilled freshly squeezed orange juice and a seat in the town square, where we watched the world go by for an hour or so, before getting the tram back to Puerto Soller.

Puerto Soller, our home for the week, was now under a blue sky. Holiday makers sat outside cafes and bars, drinking San Miguel beer, which was a good reason for us to do the same. Two couples nearby looked at us with interest as we off loaded our rucksacks and ordered 'tres cervezas grande.'

'English?' asked one of the men.

We nodded.

'You ... have ... been walking?'

'Yep.'

The two men and two women smiled, showing interest.

'Have ..... you ..... been ...far?'

Frank nodded. 'Far enough,' he said, ' for the first day.'

'How many ... hours?'

'About six,' replied Frank.

The Germans nodded. 'That is a long walk,' said the man. He said something to the others to which they all looked suitably impressed. He was the only one to speak any English, as we later found out. 'And where did you walk?'

'Up from Soller,' I said. 'Up a cobbled path.'

The Germans looked puzzled.

'Show them the map,' said Frank, 'it'll be easier.'

I delved into my rucksack for the 'Mapa Militar de Espana' number 670 at 1:50,000 scale, which I unfolded and laid out on the table top. The Germans came over and surrounded us, looking down at the map. The spokesman said something about 'Gutten karta,' to which the others were in obvious agreement.

Frank took over, pointing to Soller then tracing the route with his finger until his finger was back on Soller. 'then we got the tram back.' he said.

'That is ... amazing,' said the spokesman. 'Where did you get the map?

'London,' I replied.

'You get this Spanish Map in London?' said our new friend. He unfolded a small map of the island. It was really a road map of Mallorca. 'This is all I have.'

I don't think we ever knew the names of the Germans, but they became our friends for the remaining holiday. The spokesman always wore a small peaked cap, the type a tank commander might have had. He was known as the tank commander from then on.

As we approached our hotel, a bus pulled up, and some people shuffled off and a familiar loud voice was heard along the length of the promenade. She was back. Some of the others looked exhausted. She glared at us, as we marched into the hotel, eyeing up our rucksacks suspiciously, but did I catch change in her expression? She nodded, barely. 'Been far?' came a booming voice.

'About nine hours, the walk,' lied Frank,. making his way past her to get to the bar.

I think I noticed that her jaw dropped ever so slightly. A disbelieving frown formed itself over eyes that narrowed. 'What time did you leave here, then?'

'About six, this morning,' said Paul, 'wasn't it?'

Frank and I nodded.

'Yes, nobody around, then,' explained Frank.

She didn't want to believe us, but found it hard not to. The woman came closer. 'Got some right wimps here with me,' she said, lowering her tone but looking to see if her colleagues were within earshot. 'Some were flagging after the first five miles.'

It appeared that she was a mountaineering guide for one of the better known holiday companies, which offered packaged walking holidays on Mallorca and other places. This group had to put up with her for a full week.

That night, feeling adventurous, we had a bottle of the white wine with our meal, a fact that met the approval of the waiter who gave us that knowing wink which implied that we knew our wines. The boss lady's voice echoing round the restaurant as all in her group looked tired out and could not get a word in edgeways even if they had the inclination. Some looked as if they were about to fall asleep.

The town and its bars looked inviting. We were all thirsty after our long walk but there was enough beer in Soller to quench our thirsts. We met the tank commander and his group in one bar, then moved on to another after a few words of cracked German by us and broken English by them. Two hours later, on the way back, we met up with the Germans again. After two hours of drinking, my German and the

70

German's English had improved to the point that we understood each other much better. Alcohol does that, and without lessons. The tank commander said that they had decided to go walking the following day, and wanted to know where we were going. I told him that we were going up L'Ofra, a perfectly pointed mountain at a height of 1090 metres above sea level.

Later, as we neared our hotel, we could see the English hikers sitting outside on plastic chairs. They sipped coffee in silence under the canopy and their leader was at the bar with a glass of beer.

'Trez cervazas grande, por favor.' Paul was getting good at Spanish.

'Si.' The waiter was the one with select wine list tucked away in his brain.

'Going far tomorrow?' asked the walking guide.

''Another early one,' nodded Frank. 'That's why we're having an early night.'

The woman looked at her watch. It was nearly midnight. 'You call this early?'

'We'll just have another couple,' lied Frank, 'then we'll hit the sack.'

The woman shook her head, downed her remaining beer and moved from the bar to the stairs. 'Goodnight then.'

The brandy bottle was moved so that some of its contents could be poured into the toothbrush glass, up to the brim, then replaced, guardian of the door, where it stayed on duty throughout the night. As Frank and I climbed into bed, Paul was deeply into his sleep.

In the morning I did not hear the English group as they congregated in front of the hotel, but Frank and Paul did. I didn't really feel like getting up, never mind climb a mountain. But the planned walk was to climb up L'Ofra, the pointed mountain that had been highly visible the previous day. The idea was to get a bus to a reservoir the other side of Soller, then to walk by the reservoir, known as the Embalse de Cubar, along a path that, according to the map, led directly to the triangular mountain. The bus wove its way up the mountain road and stopped for us close to the path entrance. The sky above was blue with just a hint of cloud and the walking was easy being on the flat by the side of the reservoir. From this walk it is possible to easily reach the top of the Pilgrim steps, and I believe that the Hikers we met coming down the day before had come via this path, therefore having no uphill walking to do. From the path, by the water's edge, we could see, behind some lower hills, Mallorca's highest mountain, Puig Mayor, with its radar warning dome on the very peak. This mountain top was out of bounds to hikers. The white dome was seen fleetingly through wisps of cloud that hung about the peak like a sparse straggly grey wig. My hangover was clearing and the mood was good humoured as we made our way along the path. At one point the path leading to the top of L'Ofra, crossed through a farm field. By a stile, a sign made it perfectly clear that we had to beware of a bull presumably occupying that field. We hesitated, but there was no other path to skirt the field, therefore avoiding the bull. On the other side of the field, we could see the stile that would take us out of the field, and on to the mountain.

'There's no bull in the field,' said Frank.

Paul was more cautious. 'Oh, I don't know. It might be hiding.'

All of the field could be observed from our position, and it was definitely minus a bull.

'Maybe sometimes it does have a bull,' I said, scanning the four corners of the field.

'Or it's been seen off in a bullfight,' added Frank, smiling. 'It's not here now. Come on.'

Frank was first over the stile and into the field. I followed, and cautious Paul was close behind. We moved fast, observing no bovine presence or movement. The other stile seemed suddenly far away. Half way there, Paul swore and passed me.

'What?' I said, fearing the worst.

'Over there,' gasped Paul, picking up speed.

Then Frank saw it.

A large rocky hillock occupied a far corner of the field, and from this grey mass, a black object was peeping. The black object had two pointed horns like a devil, its body hidden by the rocks. Then more of the bull made itself known to us as it shuffled out into view, like a cartoon character. The bull was playing with us.

We all swore as the bull moved out further until its entire body was visible, motionless, and observing.

'It's not bothered,' said Frank, picking up speed.

'Is that stile nearer than the one we've just come over?' asked Paul, wondering whether or not to retreat.

The bull put its head down and a rear hoof tapped at the ground. Its head bobbed up and down. We all swore, seeing evil black eyes glinting like lasers. The bull moved forward, as did we.

The stile moved backwards, away from us as the bull neared at a canter. Swearing predominated our words and we ran to the stile. The bull danced towards us on almost delicate legs, then charged. It was twenty feet tall or taller - maybe thirty - so it seemed, and it could run like Seb Coe. Our lives were re-lived before us as the stile was suddenly there, where three people tried to get through a space made for one.

On the other side, out of the field, we fell about laughing, utter relief bringing about the humour of it all. The bull, we were sure, was also laughing from the middle of the field, from where it stood looking at us with those laser eyes. it would probably write in its diary "A good day today. Scared some hikers shitless. Ole."

We stared back at the bull, calling it some not very nice names, before carrying on towards L'Ofra. Eventually the ascent became steep as the limestone rocks became devoid of greenery, then soon we were on the almost pointed peak, looking down over most of the island.

It was from this spot that I suffered a moment of vertigo as I looked down at the three hundred and sixty degree view of Mallorca. Limestone mountains, speckled with green, predominated the view, and only the white blob on Puig Mayor seemed higher. White clouds were level with us not far away, but this is what we came to Mallorca for. Magaluf and tourists seemed a million miles away, and we supped bottled water to celebrate.

As we started the descent, a voice boomed from hell. The peace of Mallorca's mountains was shattered, and people could be seen on the path below. It was her, the Godmother. Did a bolt of lightening strike through those clouds in the distance? I searched for a crucifix, forgetting that I never carried one. But maybe the garlic on my breath from the meal last night might do the trick.

She was leading the pack of wimps up to us. Then one of her group saw us and waved, and we waved back. Some stragglers were far behind, but going at their own pace in that heat. Then she saw us, and froze momentarily realising that we were indeed hikers and up to it. She ran up to the top, as if to prove something. I got ready to breathe on her with my garlic breath.

'See you made it, then,' she said. She looked down at her trailing group, shaking her head. 'Some of this lot couldn't climb a stepladder,' she scorned.

We waited for the first of the group to arrive on the top, then said our goodbyes, before setting off back down a path.

'Can't stop,' said Frank,' we've a lot to do yet.

The woman stared at us from the peak as we moved quickly downwards. In our direction, the clouds seemed to be thickening, and mist patches were grouping everywhere. But soon we were on a lower path and the walking was easy again. Half an hour later it started to rain, and mist came from nowhere. We followed the path with the paint markings, as one should.

It is what happened next that I write with great embarrassment, and hurt pride, because I did what I am always telling people not to do. I carried on without ever looking at my compass, using intuition as my guide, but changing direction without knowing it. We walked seemingly for ever in the mist, then as quickly as it came, it cleared, in patches at first - enough to see downhill to a road.

We all agreed that that was the road we should be on to do a short walk back to Soller. We seemed to have been walking for a very long time. Then we found a path down to the road, through woods and then fields. Coming down took ages, but then we were on the road, civilisation and cars. The sun was now shining in a blue sky.

We had been walking for only a few minutes when a car pulled up. It was the tank commander and his group. 'Where are you going?' he asked.

'Soller,' we said in unison.

'That is far,' he said. 'I will give one of you a lift, then come back for the others.'

'No' we assured him. We would walk.

'Really,' The Germans shook their heads in amazement, and grinned respectfully at our determination. 'You are very fit,' were his last words before driving off with a cheerful wave.

'What does he mean, we are very fit?' asked Paul. Soller isn't far.

Frank and I frowned but said nothing as we walked towards Soller. We had walked for a half hour when an open backed farm truck pulled up, mainly because Paul had his thumb stuck out at the time.

'Soller,' said Paul, pointing ahead.

The Mallorcan shook his head. 'It... far. You ...get train. I am not going to Soller!

Train,?' said Frank.

'Si.' The man noticed that I was holding the map and he held his hand out.

Unfolding the map, then searching it for ages, the man then pointed to a position on a road coloured red. 'You here,' he said smiling.

The other two glared at me, the great explorer. I had taken then down the wrong side of the mountain, miles away from where we should have been. I could not believe it. 'You get the train,' said the man.

We all nodded in agreement.

'We get the train,' I said, embarrassed.

The sky was blue and the air was hot as we climbed into the back of the truck. Above, the mist had cleared. The other two stared at me and I stared at the floor of the truck, embarrassed. The rickety truck then made its way along the road, navigating hairpin bends. Mountains reached up to the blue sky on both sides, and I found it hard to control a feeling of nausea as I hung on for dear life.

'At least we are seeing parts of the island most tourists don't ' said Paul, in an effort to console me. The look in his eyes gave away his real thoughts.

I think that we were all slightly bruised as the truck came to a halt in a small village surrounded by hills. 'Station that way,' said the main, pointing, as we clambered on to the ground. Then he was gone, with a smile and nod.

Not much was moving in that village, so we made our way in the direction that the man had pointed and soon were at the small station that seemed deserted. All doors to the station building were closed, with no sign of life anywhere. Frank knocked on a door, then again, and again. A voice in Spanish came from somewhere, then looking up, we saw a head looking down from an open first floor window.

'When's the next train to Soller?' asked Paul.

'Two hours,' said the man, sticking two finger in the air. The head retreated back into the station building, leaving us gazing up to the sky. One could imagine Clint Eastwood, complete with poncho and half chewed cigar, leaning against that station building, waiting for someone to make his day. As for us we had two hours to kill.

Back in the village centre people were hanging about outside a small school, presumably waiting for the children to come out. The pace of things was nearly at a halt, and nobody was going to speed things up. Clint Eastwood was about to destroy the peace and quiet soon. In reality it was Paul.

A small bar was conveniently nearby, and we had two hours to ourselves. In the bar, some men, watching a bullfight on television , tore their eyes from the screen momentarily, to look at the strangers. '

Hola,' we greeted.

'Hola, 'said the Mallorcans, then turned back to the bullfight.

'Tres cervazas grande,' I said to the man behind the bar.

'Si.'

Then the peace was shattered. Paul, navigating his way to a vacant table, turned and with his rucksack, which he was in the act of off-loading from his back, knocked over about four glasses of cervazas grande. Beer was swept everywhere and men moved quicker than they'd moved in a long time. Frank put his head in his hands. I grimaced as four middle aged men got to their feet .

'Sorry,' said Paul, meekly, hoping that Clint Eastwood would come to the rescue. 'How do you say four beers?' he asked. He had not rehearsed four.

'Quatro cervazas grande,' I said.

Paul pointed to the four unjust men. 'Quatro cervazas grande,' he said,

Then the men laughed loudly. 'No problem,' said one of them, the only one in the village who knew any English. Somebody threw a cloth and the men mopped up the beer.

We sat down, embarrassed. The men were still laughing but the bullfight was more important and spilt beer was no problem. We tried to linger over our beer, but it was hot in that bar and the beer was cold. Fifteen minutes later we sauntered out into the sunlight and sat down near the school. The pace seemed to have slowed even further, if such a thing was possible. I think people were walking backwards. Frank remarked that only he had not made a mistake that day, yet. but there was time. Eventually we made our way to the spaghetti western railway. Clint Eastwood had not yet turned up but some other people had, waiting for the train that would be here, hopefully in half an hour. We sat down on the floor with our backs against the station building. After a minute or two Paul was fast asleep, and when the train approached had to be forcibly woken up. Paul fell asleep on the train after two minutes and had to be woken up in Soller.

Soller was quiet and hot. It was late afternoon and people sat around the town square, sipping beer. Among those sitting in the square was the tank commander and his group. They waved.

'How have you got here?' asked the commander.

'Walked,' said Frank.

'Ran the last few miles, actually,' added Paul, wiping his brow.

'You ran?' The commander told the others in German. They looked at us in awe. The commander summoned a waiter and asked us what we wanted to drink. A token gesture for our achievement. 'That is a very long walk.' The tank commander shook his head.

Later, after waking Paul again and then alighting from the electric tram in Puerto Soller, we saw the English hikers sitting outside our hotel. The woman guide was conspicuous by her absence and they were more talkative than usual. Some of them were bird watchers but mostly they were just hikers who had come to Mallorca just to explore the walks. Some were fit but others had expected a leisurely time, not the forced marches that they seemed to be subjected to, although being fair to the guide, I suspect that maybe they had not studied the brochure details properly.

With the evening meal, we ordered the red wine and won the waiter's approval again. That night, we toured the resort's bars again, finding some that we had missed the previous two nights. We ended up with the German foursome using the tank commander as an interpreter.

One of the days in Puerto Soller, we had as a day off. Doing nothing but getting up late, then lolling around the place, even a spot of sunbathing on the small beach. As the day progressed, we noticed that the local people were dressed up in local costumes, especially the children. Then, in the late afternoon, the peace of the resort was totally destroyed when a huge explosion echoed across the bay, bringing those at tables along the promenade to their feet and doing nasty things to three hangovers. Then another bang, like a bomb exploding, made sure that everyone was awake in Puerto Soller. Other explosions occurred high up in the mountains and people ran about, shouting like lunatics. Mallorcans crowded to the beach, pointing out to sea as an armada of small boats appeared in the opening to the bay. Men with rifles fired out to sea as the boats neared and women screamed from the shore. The air was filled with gunfire and large ear splitting bangs and the whole place had gone mad. It was one of the festivals that occurs in Mallorca, to celebrate the many battles between the Christians and the Moors. Those in the boats were the invading Moors who were about to be repelled by the victorious Christians. Then on the beach, the Moors ran on to the sand, waving swords and guns, and hand to hand combat took place before us, with many casualties on both sides. But eventually the Christians overcame the invaders and the remaining Moors beat a hasty retreat, a fact that was celebrated by much jeering and then bands played and everybody cheered. Guns fired at the retreating enemy and everybody was happy other than those who were genuinely injured in the enthusiastic pretend fighting, some with cuts and bruises from the swirling cutlasses. First aid was on hand at all times.

Sleepy Puerto Soller wasn't so sleepy after all and the bands played on. The fancy dress shop had done well, and that was the noisiest of our days in Puerto Soller.

Our next walk was to be along the cliffs. It was the walk I'd seen described in the newspaper months before, but the details of the route had been vague. But I had a map. And this time I would use it, and the compass. In fact two maps were needed this time because the intended route ended in the north east corner of one map and continued on the south west corner of another map. The start of the walk was where a country path seemed to join up with a road, some five kilometres or so from the resort. We decided to get a taxi. The taxi driver could not speak English but did understand the map and did seem to know the spot we were pointing to.

In no time at all the taxi pulled into a small clearing by a gate, to which he pointed. We had started a little later than planned and to get back to Puerto Soller, we had to get a boat from Sa Collobra. The boat always left at five o'clock in the evening and there was only one boat. My map reading had to be better than on the previous day.

Again the sky overhead was all blue as we set off along a well marked path. The walking was easy and through wonderful scenery, about six kilometres or so to the cliffs overlooking the Med. No other hikers could be seen, but somewhere along that path we had to go through a farm that sold welcoming freshly crushed orange juice. We wondered whether it was a mirage, but the Mallorcan woman who served us seemed real enough, also four German hikers were sitting there enjoying cooling drinks. The first view from the cliff edge was stunning looking out to the blue water that reached to the horizon. The path ahead was clearly marked and obviously well used, although no people could be seen. In places the sheer drop down was close to the path, but mostly tall grasses and shrubs lined the path, adding a feeling of security, as if they would stop you from falling off.

The fart was loud, very loud, the sort you could only do on a cliff edge with no-one about. I forget who did it, but it was not me. I think it was Paul. And there was no sea breeze to drag it away or hide it amongst the rustling of grasses. But it was anti-social and out of place in such a setting. Somehow destroying the serenity of it all.

To our left high grasses hid a ledge overlooking the Med, and from the high grasses, heads appeared, searching out what their ears had told them. Disapproving faces looked as if someone had broke wind at their dinner table, which was nearly true because they were having their lunch on that ledge. It was the hikers from our hotel complete with the guide who glared at us as might a Greenpeace member to an active whaling ship.

'Good afternoon,' greeted Frank. 'I wish we had time to dawdle.' We marched on towards Sa Calobra, leaving what Paul had done with the hikers.

'We're only stopping for a minute,' shouted the walking guide, almost apologetically.

We marched on but faster, just to show her. Looking back, we saw that the hikers had been motivated into action, and we speeded up even more. Ahead rocky outcrops reached out like bony fingers into the sea. Eventually as the ground dipped, we caught sight of some sand down below, then more sand, and a small bay appeared before us that surrounded blue green water. It looked like heaven.

'There's a bar down there,' said Paul, speeding up all the more. 'Look'

We looked. A small building, the only one in sight, was but metres from the sea. And there were people there, or at least there were two people there., sunbathing near the building.

'Tres San Miguel por favor,' rehearsed Paul, racing on. We followed down the hill towards the bar and civilisation. 'Tres San Miguel, por favor.' Paul was at the sand with us close behind. The afternoon sun beat down on us but soon we would have ice cold beer in a heavenly setting. The bar grew nearer and the sand was hard to run on in hiking boots.

Paul had stopped. 'I don't believe it.'

'What?' I asked, fearing the worst.

Frank had stopped running behind me. 'What's the matter?'

'The place is deserted. And it's not a bar, anyway.' Paul sank to his knees on the sand. 'All that sweating for nothing,' Disconsolate, he looked out to sea, like a shipwrecked mariner on a desert island. But that's how we all felt. I yanked a bottle of water from my rucksack, took a mouthful then spit out the hot liquid. We all swore with great enthusiasm and venom, and stared out to sea. The little bay full of blue water, and the Mediterranean beyond looked wonderful but would have looked more wonderful with a large ice cold beer in my hand. But we still had to get to Sa Calobra, from where the boat would leave at five o'clock. It was nearly four o'clock and Sa Calobra was about three or four kilometres away. Enough time to walk, but we needed cold drinks.

Inland, a track led to Sa Calobra and on that track a taxi stood as if waiting for us. Next to the taxi, an industrial tractor with a large bucket attachment stood idly by. A miracle. The taxi driver had to be woken up from his siesta, then minutes later we in Sa Calobra, and the nearest bar, where I consumed a large bottleful of fizzy mineral water, with lots of ice, in a matter of seconds. We had plenty of time for another drink.

The boat was there waiting for us, when the tractor pulled up with its human cargo in its bucket, her-who-shall-be-obeyed with some of her group. The bucket lowered to the ground and the human cargo spilled out near the jetty. Then the tractor went back for the others. The guide strode up to the boat issuing orders to the Mallorcan who was collecting the fares.

'There's quite a few of us,' she said to man. 'So I think we can do a deal. Let's call it a group booking, therefore a discount would be quite in order. There's my group of ten, plus these three.' The guide looked over at us as we were about to board the boat.

The Mallorcan looked at her as he might do to a hole in his boat. 'No discount lady. We don't do discounts.' With a bored expression the boat's captain turned to us and we offered him our money, the correct number of pesetas.

'Well we're not paying the full money. What about ten percent discount?' we heard her say.

'What about you stay in Sa Calobra,' we heard the man say.

'But you'll have an empty boat,'

'And you'll be in Sa Calobra. We leave soon.' His script sounded as if it had been written for Groucho Marx.

Eventually the other hikers were delivered in the tractor bucket and made their guide see sense. They paid the full amount and boarded the boat, but under protest from the guide.

I don't like boat journeys, even comparatively short ones like this, and the smell of the diesel fuel didn't help as the boat did the return trip to Puerto Soller. But the scenery made it all worthwhile. The cliffs looked awesome from this close range and we could retrace our walk along the top, although it was hard to believe that a path existed somewhere up there among what appeared to be barren rocky ledges. Paul was asleep in minutes, something I tried but the boat's movement and the smell made me feel sick. The view was something else but I wanted to get on dry land as soon as possible. Eventually a black and white striped lighthouse told us that we were nearly there, and then we were in the bay looking at the coastline with the hotels on the front and other white buildings dotting the lower hills. The backdrop was of limestone mountains with blue sky above. Dry land was getting nearer and Paul was still asleep. I felt like a Moor invading the Island and hoped there were no canons to fire at us as we neared the jetty and dry land.

For the last big walk we did, we are indebted to a certain Archduke Louis Salvador who, in the late nineteenth century, bought a chunk of Mallorca's coastline near Valldemosa, because of the fine walks and stunning views it offered. The Archduke built paths and had favourite viewpoints along these paths, on which he spent much of his time. The paths are now looked after by ICONA, who do a wonderful job of maintaining them and painting the little red dots that guide us hikers from falling off steep cliffs. ICONA also maintain restorations of charcoal burners huts along this path, and other marvellous reminders of Mallorca's past. The manufacture of charcoal was once an important part of Mallorcan life but died out when other fuels took over.

Half the battle, I always think, especially when abroad and starting off on a hike, is finding the beginning of a walk. It's usually reasonably easy once your up on the hills or in open country, but getting started can usually be a pain. From the bus station at Valldemosa we walked to where we considered the walk should start but struggled to find it. Then a man, in dressing gown and slippers, carrying his morning newspapers stopped in his tracks when he saw our puzzled expressions. Our Mapa Militar de Espania gave us no clues to the start of our walk, only a vague direction. The man could speak no English and grimaced when he saw the map.

'The Archduke's path,' I said hoping. That did the trick. The man did a turn of direction and beckoned us to follow him to a path that we reached after a few minutes. He pointed, smiled and left to enjoy his breakfast, and us to enjoy the start of the walk which was on a stony path. The path led up through a wooded area then along the higher parts from which we climbed to the top of a mountain called Teix at a height of 1062 metres then re-joined the path. The views again were stunning as the path got very near to the edge which overlooked the lower speckled hills and the sea. Re-tracing the old Archduke's steps, we could appreciate why he thought so much of the place. Many interesting sights made the walk something special, such as the charcoal burners huts, a chapel built in a cave, and other sights one would never see from the trappings of tourism   which seemed so far away. This walk seems to be one of the most famous on the island and is featured in all the walking guides to Mallorca that I have since read. Full marks to the Archduke and to ICONA for keeping up the good work. The walk, a true circular route, took us back to Valldemosa, a lovely town, once the home of Frederick Chopin, and birthplace of the Island's saint, Catalina Thomas, who's body is preserved in Palma.

Later, in the darkness of our bedroom, after a night on the town, the wardrobe door moved again with a rusty creak, to disturb our slumbers. But by that time, the bottle was devoid of its contents, therefore lacking in ballast, allowing the door to move.

Waiting for the coach on the last day in Puerto Soller, Frank, in shades and blazer, looked the part of a tanned James Bond, who had gone through the hotel's wine list three times.

Looking at the maps, it was obvious that there was a lot more of Mallorca to explore, and as I said goodbye to the horses standing at the hotel front, waiting patiently by their carriages, I vowed to return and explore some more of Mallorca's hills.

At Manchester Airport, Frank was the only one on our plane to have his luggage searched, mind you it was easy to regard him as some international terrorist, with his shades and blazer. I think they thought he was Carlos the Jackal, not Frank the precision engineer.

I would definitely recommend Mallorca for a walking holiday, with its large areas of open country, friendly people, inexpensive hotels and restaurants, and in most cases easy to reach methods of transport. But don't go walking there in the middle of summer when it's too hot. And keep away from farmhouse dogs, something I had forgotten to include up to now. We encountered three or four farmhouses with enormous black dogs on long chains fixed near to the farmhouse doors. It is obvious that Mallorcan farmers have learned how to cross Rottweilers with sabre-toothed tigers. These devil dogs from hell, we found would not bark until unwary hikers were within a close distance to the farms, then they would spring out like greyhounds from the traps, bearing great teeth dripping with saliva and somebody's blood. The chains would be just long enough to allow the dogs to reach the farmhouse gate and no further. Then, the dogs, racing so fast, would raise up in the air then fall back as if on elastic. One farmhouse actually had two of these monsters, one on either side of the door, and both of them came at us from two directions and finished up crashing into each other. Once, I think it was the first time we encountered one of these beasts, we approached this farm, and the dog began to whine and whimper like a baby, then ran into its kennel, from where it peered out, still whining. Frank commented on the cowardice of the beast, and we marched on, laughing. The dog must have judged exactly when we were nearest to the extent of the chain, because at that point, the timid wreck became a snarling maniac and flew at us with glinting teeth bared and mad black eyes. Needless to say, we were frightened to death until we realised the chain's restraint. Then the air was blue. We commented on the evil cunning of the beast, but from then on, we were ever cautious when approaching farms and hoped that Mallorcan chains were very strong. So, when you are walking in Mallorca, beware of the dogs as well as the bulls.

7   MALLORCA 2

When Alan Rayner saw my Mallorcan photographs he decided to come with me to the holiday isle the following year. We opted to stay in Puerto Pollenca this time, a holiday village and fishing port to the north of the island, with a reputation of having one of the best bays in the Mediterranean. Needless to say, it also had many bars and restaurants to explore, and was handy for getting to the start of a lot of Mallorca's best walks. This holiday has many amusing memories which seemed to happen from day one, although in some ways the trip was a bit anticlimactic as going to the same place twice sometimes can be. Also, unlike the first time, the weather was terrible for most of the time. Much of the fun on this trip had very little to do with walking.

The two star hotel we chose was similar to the previous year's hotel, and was staffed by Basil Fawlty impersonators who did it without trying. The waiters were openly hostile and twice tried to pick fights with us but were instantly quelled with Alan's don't mess with me, I'm from Eccles look, which reduced them to quivering fools. Sharing our hotel was a group of old people from a care home in Birmingham who were being looked after by four women carers with the patience of saints and the humour of Les Dawson. Most of those being cared for seemed to be suffering from some sort of senile dementia, and didn't appear to know where they were for most of the time. But the carers were magnificent, taking their charges everywhere, sightseeing, on the beach, even disco dancing.

It's easy to see why Puerto Pollenca has become such a tourist attraction, with its sandy beach to the front of a tree lined promenade, its yacht harbour, many art galleries, antique shops, and all of it without the brazen nightlife of louder resorts. A bit boring you might say. Alan and myself were the only lager louts in the place. And everywhere you look, mountains peer down at you from the blue sky. Well, sometimes it's blue.

As usual, I had pre-planned some walks, but this time it did not all happen as planned, and for the first time met some hostility from Mallorcan landowners.

Just as Puerto Soller had Soller nearby, Puerto Pollenca has Pollenca nearby, and from this much-visited town there are the start of many good walks. Pollenca is surrounded by orchards, farms and mountains, as are most places on that side of the isle, and in its centre, you can idle your time away in the Plaza Major by the church. A famous Roman bridge spans the Torrente Sant Jordi River, and Agatha Christie used the town as the setting for one of her books.

I can't remember the order of things, but on one walk I had planned, we met opposition after the first twenty minutes, and not far from Pollenca. We had to get to the bridge to find our bearings, and Alan had been going to night school to learn Spanish. 'La Puente Romana, por favor,' he said to an approaching Mallorcan grandmother in black. The woman looked at him blandly and nodded behind us. The bridge was but yards away. 'Gracias,' he said. It was like asking her where the floor was.

'That was really helpful,' I said.

Alan told me to shut up as we marched on. Finding the start of this walk was easy, but then ahead we could hear raised voices, English and Spanish. As we approached the English voices were raised higher and shrill.

A small table stood across the path. On the other side, a middle aged Mallorcan man, sitting on a chair, was shaking his head . Two empty San Miguel bottles stood idly by on the table, and two full ones stood waiting to be opened. An ash tray contained more cigarette butts than he could have smoked and more lay on the ground.

On our side of the table, six people, three men and three women, were all talking at once. 'You can't stop us,' said one of the men, in slightly effeminate voice.

'Yes I can,' said the Mallorcan, before lighting a cigarette, and blowing smoke at the Englishman.

'Trouble at t'mill?' asked Alan as we stopped some few feet from the argument.

'This man is refusing to let us through,' said the Englishman, 'and he can't do that.'

There was something about the Englishman's voice that I disliked immensely. It wasn't just what he said, but the way he said it - a certain arrogance, that only some Englishmen possess. And effeminate.

_ 'I think he can,' said Alan.

'We have the right,' said the man,' to go on any path on the island that leads to the sea. It's the law of the land. And this path leads to the sea.' The tone of his voice made me cringe. But the man at the table was having none of it. And neither would I

'What's the problem?' asked Alan, to the Mallorcan.

The man shrugged. He then explained in the best English that he could muster, that his boss, who owned the land on which this path happened to be on, was fed up of having his peace disturbed by foreign hikers. The path, he said passed his bosses house, and today, his boss wanted some peace from the hikers. But we could go on the path if we were off it again by a certain time. The time he gave us, gave us no chance to complete our intended walk.

The Englishman was becoming more arrogant, which was not the way to get anywhere in this argument and the Mallorcan had stopped listening anyway. We took the only course of action and left them all to it, knowing that there was no way we were going to walk where we had intended. As we walked away we could here the Englishman telling the Mallorcan that he could not stop people on the path, and that it was all ridiculous. Ridiculous or not, everybody was going nowhere fast. We moved out of earshot and made further plans. In any case, maybe fate had taken a hand in our affairs, because the sky was becoming grey and the mountain tops were quickly disappearing from view behind dark clouds. I had seen the signs a thousand times before. Then I did detect fine specks of rain on my face. Oh well, Alan and myself should be used to all this. After all we had been back packing in Iceland. We reverted to plan 'B', not that we had a plan 'B' when we started out. On the other side of Pollenca from our intended walk is The Puig de Maria, which is a steep hill with a convent sanctuary on top. We decided that, under the circumstance, the Puig de Maria was plan 'B' The sanctuary was probably the easiest place yet to find because it is the only steep hill so close to the town.

I believe that every Easter Monday, thousands of locals make that slog up to the sanctuary, and most Sundays there are many people up there. But in the rain, mid week, we encountered no-one as we trudged up the cobbled path to the steps leading to the courtyard of the sanctuary. All the way up, Alan cursed the arrogant Englishman, the Mallorcan landowner and the weather. If I hadn't been out of breath, I would have joined in. As it happened, I just nodded to let him know that I agreed with him.

The view from the top should have been spectacular, but all we could see was the faint dots of Pollensa's white buildings showing like ghosts through a mist. the rest of Mallorca was just guesswork in the distance. I imagine that on a sunny, clear day much of the island can be seen. Then we were able to buy a cup of coffee at the sanctuary before trudging down again in heavy rain. A very anticlimactic day up to now, then we got the bus back to Puerto Pollenca and the residents of the Birmingham care home who managed to cheer us up without knowing it.

As the bus neared Puerto Pollenca, the sky got bluer and the day warmed up, and because of this Puerto Pollensa was a cheerier place than Pollenca had been. Back at the hotel, people were turning out around the small swimming pool and it all looked as Mallorca is expected to look. The carers had organised their charges on deck chairs and sun beds around the pool, and Alan and myself flopped down amongst them, dropping our rucksacks on the tiled ground. The carers then introduced us to those in their care, a magic moment..

One of the them, an old chap who wore a cap all the time, who we'll call Albert, came and sat with us. After our introduction, Albert got excited, and jumped to his feet, waving frantically to some point above him. We all looked up, seeing nothing but blue sky and a plane which had probably had just taken off from Palma airport on the other side of the island. Albert waved happily, then shouted; 'It's me, Albert.'

One of the cares explained. 'He knows all the pilots,' she said, 'Don't you, Albert?'

'Shut up, I'm waving to my mate,' scolded Albert, pointing skywards.

Then Albert turned to Alan and myself: 'I know him, you know. Did you see him waving back at me?'

'Course we did,' agreed Alan. 'How do you know him?'

'Never mind that,' said Albert. 'I know them all.'

'He does,' said a carer, nodding.

'And they always wave,' added Albert. The plane had quickly gone from overhead and Albert asked if he could have a drink of beer. The carer took him away to the bar, from where he returned, smiling with a glass of cold Spanish ale. But before long, another plane appeared in the sky and Albert got a carer to hold his glass so that he could wave to another of his mates. That afternoon he must have waved to twenty pilots who obviously waved back.

'He's got lots of mates, has Albert,' explained a carer.

Albert nodded. 'I used to fly with most of them, in the RAF!'

Well that explained why Albert knew all the pilots, and we did not need to ask again, but he must have waved to hundreds of his old buddies over the week. A popular man was Albert, who thought he was in Blackpool.

Later, before the evening meal, Alan and I decided to have a lie down in our room. Alan was studying the map for the next day's walk. and I began to drift into a relaxed sleep. I don't know how long I'd been out when a gentle voice close to me spoke. At first I thought it was in my subconscious but the voice spoke again.

'Hello, what are you doing in my room?'

My slowly opening eyes looked into a kind old face only inches from mine. I realised that it was all real, and heard Alan speak from the other bed.

'Who's that? Have you trapped off?'

'I don't mind you being in my room,' said the old woman on my bed.

I sat up. 'Hello,' I said.

'Hello,' said the old woman. 'How long have you been here?'

'A couple of days?'

'How strange,' said the woman. 'I hope you don't mind if I lie down, I'm tired.'

'Not at all,' I said.

'Thank you. It's nice here, isn't it?'

'Yes it is,' I said.

'You have trapped off,' said Alan from his bed.

'Oh, there's two of you,' said the old woman. 'But you can stay here if you want.'

The old woman must have been there in our room for five minutes when much shouting could be heard from the corridor, through the part opened door.

'She's in here,' shouted Alan.

_ Then the door opened fully and two relieved carers came into our room. 'There you are,' sighed one of them. Thank God. How long has she been here?'

'Leave her, my mate's trapped off.' said Alan.

'She's always going missing,' said one of the carers. 'Yesterday she got on a bus to Palma.'

They gently eased the old woman off my bed and led here out of the room. 'Sorry about this,' said one of the carers, shutting the door behind her.

Alan made threats to tell Sylvia when we got home. I made sure the door was closed properly then re-visited the land of nod for an hour.

Puerto Pollenca was fairly quite at that time of the year, and we found a bar on the front where we quickly made friends with the owner, mainly because we were usually the only ones in the place. Alan would try out his Spanish on the man and I learned how to ask for the bill.

On one of our walks we encountered what appeared to be wild pigs living in an orchard, and we had to walk through this grunting, chomping group to continue on our way, but the pigs seemed preoccupied with their dinner and I don't think they even noticed us. Someone who did notice us though was a man, to our left, looking over a fence that surrounded a large house with plenty of grounds. A couple of handsome horses strutted across the grounds, and the man gestured for us to keep going. The shotgun he held was incentive enough, and we did not falter in our tracks. On the ground were many spent shotgun cartridges, and it was a wonder the pigs hadn't eaten some of them. Maybe they had. Maybe the man thought that we were going to pinch some apples, or squeeze a pig or two into our rucksacks. I don't like my rucksack to be too heavy, so we left the pigs chomping, but I must be honest - the real reason was the shotgun. It would have been nice to have had a good English breakfast with plenty of bacon, even if it did contain hundreds of small lead balls. But it was a good long walk and again in dull conditions, which culminated in us getting to the peak of a mountain called Puig d'es Ca, from which we could see Pollenca below and the Puig de Maria, our earlier walk, protruding upward, like a woman's breast. Beyond, the Mediterranean Sea looked grey and cold. The mountain range to our north was where we should have walked before getting stopped by the man at the table. Right behind Pollenca, sticking out into the Med, was a rocky promontory, probably the most northerly part of Mallorca, and in between was Puerto Pollenca with a handful of British dementia patients running riot. The sea was joined up to the sky as if there was no horizon, and Albert would not have been able to wave to his mates in the sky with all that low cloud.

That night, after a late meal, we sauntered into one of the posher hotels not far from where we were staying. There was a disco going on but the dance floor was empty. Alan and myself got to the bar, ordered beer, and sat down, the thing to do after a long day's walking,, then we engaged in conversation discussing the day's events. Some time later, probably after our third beer, on the way back from the toilet, and oblivious of what was going on around me, I was pushed onto the dance floor.

'You dance with them. I've had enough,' a British carer moved off to the bar.

Alan Rayner was in hysterics at our table. I was surrounded by a handful of dementia patents, who all thought they were in Blackpool, and all wandering off in different directions. A conga would have been great fun. Albert, with his cap on, looked skywards but to no avail. With tired legs I swayed to the music, and realised that those around me were moving a lot better than I was. I tried to escape but was shouted back on to the dance floor. This was embarrassing. But not as embarrassing as when I sat down.

A man at a nearby table came over and sat down at ours. 'Aren't you Alan Butterworth?'

I looked at the man, whom I did not know. 'Yes,' I cringed.

'I've got a mate who lives facing you in Failsworth.'

I reddened quickly. This man was a friend of my neighbour and good pal, Barney Phillips, who will feature later in this book. Barney lives facing me and is the biggest Mickey taker around.

'Nice mover,' said the man. 'wait till I tell Barney.' I could not believe it. The only person to know me, turns up when I'm on the dance floor with Albert and his pals. 'This must be grab-a-granny's granny night.'

Alan Rayner never let me forget that night.

There are so many good walks around that part of Mallorca, and for some you do not have to go very far, in fact in and around the nearby hills, seen from the Promenade at Puerto Pollenca, can provide some excellent walks. A good example is the Boquer valley just north of Puerto Pollenca.

This lovely walk is through a valley which is separated from the quiet holiday resort of Cala San Vicente by the Cavall Bernat ridge which has very steep cliffs dropping down on the Cala San Vicente Bay side. The Boquer valley is an easy but attractive walk to the coast with its small rocky beach that looks out to a spectacular view. Looking out to the rocky bay, you can be anywhere in the world and you could imagine Neptune wading out of those blue waters with his trident. It's the place of myths and legends. And you won't meet many people other than birdwatchers, usually somewhere near the path, with their enormous telescopes and cameras pointing usually at the Cavall Bernat ridge that is a temporary home to migrant birds. And migrant birds, Alan reckons are the only ones who should be up there on the ridge, because we climbed up to the ridge top and it is the first time I have ever known Alan have a bout of vertigo, so we came down again. Birdwatchers watched our every move through gigantic lenses. But again, a part of Mallorca that the average tourist never sees, and well worth a visit, whether on a walking holiday or not.

8   BARNEY

The mention of vertigo now brings me to the subject of Barney, husband to the long suffering Pat, and my good mate and neighbour, who has been walking with me now for many years. Going back to about 1976 with its hot summer, by which time Barney had already accompanied me on numerous walks in the Peak District and the Lakes. To Barney I had been extolling the virtues of Wasdale as my favourite place, when somehow we found ourselves organising a long weekend there. The long suffering Pat, or My Patricia, as she is sometimes called by Barney, declined the offer, but Sylvia was eager to join in. Also we took nine children, my three, Barney's two, Barney's two nephews, and two girls who were the daughters of neighbours and my daughters pals. It was a holiday to remember for if nothing else that my youngest daughter Karen, twelve then, had a close encounter of the waspy kind whilst having a wee.

Barney had had a start to his working life something akin to mine, having been brought up in Clayton, he served an engineering apprenticeship at the Mather and Platt factory in north Manchester. Mathers, as it was known, eventually became a casualty of Britain's decline where manufacturing was concerned and most of the original buildings no longer exist. At twenty-two he moved to A.V. Roe, now British Aerospace, building aeroplanes, but at thirty two moved to his true vocation.

Barney, tired of the factory life, sought a career on the markets of Greater Manchester. He now, and has done for most of his working life, sells women's clothes, on Altrincham, Sandbach and Middleton markets, a career that was always made for the likes of Barney, who is basically a people person, not that My Patricia would always agree.

Barney is a strong walker, with legs like tree trunks, but with zero tolerance of heights over a couple of feet, and an unbelievable ability to bring the worst out of country animals. I think all animals hate him and I sympathise with the dumb beasts.

Once coming across Bleaklow in Derbyshire, a ram watched us approach from the heather by the side of our path. Usually they run away, like the timid beasts they are, but not this one, obviously of sterner stuff. The ram pretended to graze, which is mostly what you see them doing. Then as we were within yards, as if Barney had mentioned mint sauce, the dumb animal charged at my friend knocking him to the ground, under a cloud of expletives from him and much laughter from me. I bet that the ram didn't know that it was such a swear word but it was learning fast. It was hate at first sight, and I wondered if the ram had been trained by 'My Patricia.'

Another time, we had been walking in the Langdale area of the Lake District, heading for Langdale Fell. We were walking along a path with a dry stone wall to one side and an open field to the other, and in the field a couple of shire horses grazed quietly at the far end. Then one of the horses, the biggest, sauntered over to us, taking its time as if time meant nothing. 'How's my old pal,' said Barney, as the massive creature neared. 'He's a good lad.'

The gentle giant closed in very slowly bending its head down - an act of total submission. 'He's my mate,' said Barney, stroking the horse's large brow. 'He's a belter.'

The horse's head was soon under Barney's armpit while my mate ruffled the animal's mane, which was the last act my pal did. The horse's head then shot up, taking Barney with it, lifting him with effortless ease off the ground, then dumping him on his backside with a thud. The horse then made one of those toothy grins that horses are famous for and galloped of with horsy laughter filling the air. To my astonishment Barney swore a lot, but I laughed a lot to compensate. I think I had heard a Bleaklow ram described with similar vocabulary, and I wondered if the two animals knew each other. I wonder how Barney would have coped with the bulls and the hounds from hell in Mallorca.

But Barney is good company on the hills, and we've sometimes been laughing that much that we've had to stop walking as the dialogue has got completely out of hand.

On the Wasdale trip, we had four tents which we pitched on the campsite at Wasdale Head, and the weather was glorious for the entire stay. The youngest of the children was six, the oldest fourteen, but Barney and myself were the biggest children for miles. Barney and I were the chefs and we cooked some inventive concoctions mainly by tipping the contents of whatever tins were at hand into a large pan, mixing them together, and then warming them up over the camping stove. Spaghetti, baked beans, boiled potatoes, Spam and whatever, mixed as one with a large spoon becomes an orange coloured collage

A very wet serial hiller before Gore-Tex.
Somewhere over Windermere. Circa 1965.

Potential serial hillers learning rope-craft on the
gateposts at the Outwood Bound School. I'm to
the front, second from the right. 1959

Alan Rayner skips across Striding Edge.
Peter is not so sure

Iceland, 1984. Serial hillers on the move

Iceland, 1984. Midnight in Iceland.
Alan Rayner marvels at the scene.

Mallorca. The cliff tops looked awesome from the
boat back to Soller.

Mallorca. Me and Paul; on the top of L'Ofra.
1090 above sea level.

Madeira 1990. A pointed peak above
stepped mountainside. The higher
mountains are shrouded in mist.
Everything is so steep.

Barney surveys the north side of the
Wilder Kaiser from the Zahmer Kaiser.

The Wilder Kaiser. Everywhere you look
it's there. That high col to the centre
is the Door of Elmau.

Barney surveys the north side of the
Wilder Kaiser from the Zahmer Kaiser.

The Wilder Kaiser. Everywhere you look
it's there. That high col to the centre
is the Door of Elmau.

to be dolloped on to tin plates which are easy to clean in the stream. Anybody who complained didn't eat. Sylvia cleaned up afterwards.

On one walk, we all, children included, went up to Burnmoor Tarn, where we picnicked by the water's edge, and some of the children paddled in the shallow, cool water of the tarn. It was one of those carefree days when nothing mattered but having a good time. We, the adults, sat on the grass watching the children playing in the tarn which was surrounded by a vast expanse of countryside with no other people in sight, as if the place was ours, and many large dragonflies winged over the tarn as our only companions. Barney, sitting on a rock by the tarn edge, read a book, and I fell asleep as the kids splashed in the water under the watchful eyes of Sylvia. These are the times to remember and the word idyllic springs to mind.

We must have stayed there for an hour or two, before making our way down the path back to the campsite, and it was on this downhill trip that Karen and her mate Tracy, decided to go into a field to answer a call of nature. The two girls had only been gone for a minute when the hills were alive with loud, frantic screams echoing from the field. The two girls then could be seen, running towards us, pulling up their jeans, with a swarm of wasps in hot pursuit. The girls had squatted directly over the wasp's nest, spraying the wasps with wee, disturbing their waspy siesta. The wasps retaliated by attacking the looming bare bottoms. Later, Sylvia bathed the girls with TCP and counted dozens of sting marks. The boys considered it very funny, but Karen and Tracy thought different.

Wasdale, as I've said before, is a place of many moods, however for most of those few days, the sun shone down on us, but of course with mist to hide the mountain tops as a start to most days. The mist usually cleared, leaving the mountains to cast shadows over the fells as the sun moved across the sky, until the moon appeared and with it the place changed again. Wasdale in moonlight, on a cloudless night is a place of watery silver surfaces below and sharp edged black mountain tops above. Misty nights make it a haunted place, where devils roam, especially when walking back to the camp site from the pub, with nine giggling children after too many Newcastle Brown ales.

One morning after breakfast, I had planned to take the boys up Yewbarrow, that rocky spine to the north of Waste Water, one of my favourite short walks, which I think is underrated, probably because it is surrounded by all the more famous ones: Pillar, Scarfell, Great Gable and the like. Although the view from the Great Door on Yewbarrow, of the Scarfells, does feature in lots of books about the Lake District.

That morning started out with clear views all around. I think we walked along the road from the camp site to the southern end of Yewbarrow to where the path starts just before Overbeck Bridge. Then suddenly a mist took over and the hilltops hid from view behind it. We walked along the easy path in the valley to west of Yewbarrow climbing gradually to Dore Head where we turned to start the steep bit up to Yewbarrow. The mist was hazy and we were in good spirits, helping the younger ones with the scrambling, but then, suddenly the mist cleared, allowing us to see down into Mosedale Beck below. Now Barney had been fine up to then, walking on that lower path, and even up the latter steep bit, he did not seem to have a problem. Steven, the younger of Barney's nephews, who was seven at the time, and had been born with one foot turned inwards, and was wearing football boots, kept up with the rest of us without any trouble. He has since had operations on that foot and now at thirty one, one would never know that he has ever had a problem.

'Oh look,' said one of the kids, pointing down to the beck. Barney nearly fainted. The green valley below unfolded quickly and Barney's eyes bulged at the sight. He sank down on his knees as if praying then stared at the ground as a torrent of abuse began to thunder across Dore Head and up and over Yewbarrow.

'What's up, Uncle Barney?' asked a nephew.

Barney cursed with the most enthusiastic venom I probably have ever witnessed, and it was only then that I knew he had a severe problem with heights.

'Oh, come here, Steven, you can't go up there, you'll get killed.' he shouted to his nephew who was enjoying the walk.

Steven, without a problem in the world, looked down at his uncle who clutched the ground with frantic fingers. 'I'm Okay, Uncle Barney.'

'No, you're not. You're not going any further. 'Oh., my God!' More Anglo Saxon obscenities wafted across the hills as would the wind.

Barney had got closer to the ground, and when he looked sideways and down, he cursed loudly.

'Come on Dad,' urged son Paul.

'I can't go on,' hissed Barney. 'I'm going to die.'

Barney decided that he could not go up, but when faced with the alternative, decided that he couldn't go down either. In fact he was stuck and was neither up nor down Yewbarrow. The boys were furious and wanted to continue, but I had to make the decision to call it a day - going upwards anyway. However, getting Barney down was harder than it sounded and at first he wouldn't budge.

'You'll have to move,' I said, but Barney called me what he had called a shire horse in Langdale and a ram on Bleaklow, or something similar. Barney did eventually get down on his bottom, without it ever leaving the ground. It took ages, but some half hour later, back on the lower path, it took him nearly as long to recover. In fact I don't think he did recover until his first pint of Newcastle Brown ale later that night.

Vertigo is a funny thing, or at least the vertigo that Barney suffers with is. He can be all right one minute, then, without any sign of danger, he goes all funny at the slightest thing. Even the thought of someone else in danger can set him off. Barney is also colour blind, so the different shades of browns and greens on Ordnance Survey maps mean nothing to him. In fact I don't know why he bothers going on the hills with all his afflictions. He is the only person I know who can get dizzy looking up a cliff, or can get in a cold sweat looking at someone standing too near what he considers to be a dangerously steep drop, as happened on our second trip to Austria, when we were walking a ridge on the Wilder Kaiser mountain range. Barney will feature in a later chapter dedicated to Austria, which did have severely precipitous drops down.

9   WHERE WATER RUNS UP HILLS

Madeira is a small volcanic island some 500 kilometres west of Africa. It consists mainly of high peaks, deep ravines and a plateau, high up in the sky. It is a magic place where water appears to run uphill through narrow canals called levados, which meander through lush vegetation and sometimes by the sides of vertiginous drops that Barney would not appreciate. It is a magic place, where cruise ships call in-between other stops, to discharge their passengers on to the streets of Funchal, the capital. It is a place where Reid's Hotel, one of the world's most famous, takes one back in time with its quiet luxury, including the serving of afternoon tea with great decorum. Reid's was built by a Scot, opened in 1891 and is not the place to tramp through with muddy hiking boots.

Madeira does not have any sandy beaches but some hotels, over thirty percent of which are of the five star class, are built on the rocks overlooking dramatic seascapes and the Atlantic Ocean. Funchal is where it's all happening, but it's all happening, where hiking is concerned, everywhere on the island, especially on the higher places, looking down sheer drops, over lush greenery resembling tropical rain forests. Steep, stepped slopes, on which farmers toil, overlook fertile valleys, and those magic levados run everywhere - like arteries spreading life water to all parts of the island. And colours prevail with the natural vegetation having been able to thrive because of the island's mild, year round climate. The place is a botanist's dream, but even if botany is not your thing, you can't help but notice, as a hiker, the wonderful exotic trees and plants as you walk all levels of the island.

Alan Rayner and myself visited Madeira twice, the first time in 1990 .That first time, as we were landing at the island's airport, the plane's captain made a joke about the passenger's helping him put the breaks on by digging our heels into the tarmac because the runway was not quite long enough to land properly. He wasn't joking.

Our hotel, a real old world Portuguese style place at the back of Funchal (We couldn't afford Reid's or the Sheraton) was just what we needed as hikers. Everything in Madeira is up or down a hill, and the hike from the capital's sea front, where the bars and restaurants are, turned out to be hard work after a night on the town, especially after a day of proper hiking. Maybe it was our imagination but all the local people seemed to have well developed calf muscles, and that was from just getting to and from work. The bus station in Funchal is down near the coast, by the side of a market, and most mornings Alan and myself would walk downhill to catch a bus somewhere. This was usually as the local population were going to work, so we would be among the crowds - office bound, therefore observing the rear leg view of secretaries and shop girls purely from the scientific view of observers of nature and human anatomy.

Our hotel room had a balcony overlooking back alleys and narrow streets below and a stunning view above of the mountains. Below, we could witness Madeirans going about their business, and above we could see that houses had been built on every possible site until steepness decided otherwise. At night, in clear weather, lights twinkled everywhere above, and below from houses and street lights. We consumed a full bottle of Chevas Regal whisky on that balcony and it was a good place to air our disgusting hiking socks and boots. It was also a good place to study the map for the next day's walk.

Now, there are, just like other countries, enough books to extol the virtues of Madeira, from the point of view of its holiday potential, regarding general tourism or those that specialise in walking and climbing, so in these pages, that side of things have been kept to a minimum. Needless to say, though, Madeira is a wonderful place, full of everything, but for walkers it's an amazing place with the most stupendous views that words or even photographs never really do justice. The best word that I can use is "different". because you would be tested to find anything like it within such near distance from Britain. You have to go and see for yourself. Even if you are not experienced walkers, get a taxi to the highest places, sometimes above the clouds, and wonder at the views. If you are a walker, buy a guidebook and a map, and see for yourself.

Our walks were all amazing experiences, sometimes accompanied by frightening views down, but gentle walks are there for the doing, and some start right from the capital, so you could begin them not far from your hotel front door.

One of our walks included a section which took in a coastal path that was described in one of the guide books as "sometimes impassable due to landslides" and "danger of vertigo." The book wasn't kidding, but this turned out to be a lovely walk and thankfully done in good weather. The part that stands out in my mind was when I first saw the bit that included the coastal path. We had got a bus from Funchal, then the walk itself began by a gentle climb uphill. After about two hours or so a headland came into view and my heart sank. At first I could not see the path, then an agonising few minutes later, an horizontal, pencil thin line became apparent somewhere a third of the way down what appeared to be a vertical cliff face. The unprotected drop down from the path to the Atlantic was 350m.

'We'll never cross that,' I said, after swearing with some passion. I sank to the ground as an excuse to stop for a meal break and take stock and possibly bring plan B into operation, whatever plan B was.

Alan looked ahead at the pencil line but showed no emotion. 'It'll be all right,' he said after a while. 'We'll manage it.'

At the time, I wished he wouldn't have said that. I took out my sandwiches for comfort and nibbled them with a sickly feeling in my stomach, my eyes not leaving the path. No, never, I convinced myself, never. 'Never, in a million years,' I sighed.

'Don't exaggerate,' scolded Alan. 'You've done worse.'

'In my dreams,' I replied, 'or nightmares.' The cheese sandwich tasted of bile.

Alan took no time to eat his sandwich, then moved off, nearer that dreaded non-existent path overlooking a horrible death on razor sharp rocks which were being hounded by roaring waves. But he looked confident. I crumpled up the wrapping paper, stuck it in my rucksack, and got to my feet on jelly legs. We had to be at a certain place for a certain time to get a certain bus back to Funchal. Alan reminded me of this as he walked off to his certain death ahead. I shook my head and followed, wondering what colourful language Barney would have used in this situation. I felt a great affinity with Barney, and began using his language to myself.

Alan was getting further away from me and I shouted for him to wait. He appeared to be clinging to a vertical surface without any visible means of support, just like a fly. I felt like crying.

'It's easy,' I heard Alan shout from the edge of nothing. 'Come on.'

I had to believe him and so I ventured forth. The thought of Barney on that ledge made me giggle, I think it's called fear. Alan waited for me, a kind gesture, which enabled him to see the fear in my face from close up.

'See, it's not so bad,' said Alan as I caught him up on a ledge that protruded about four feet from the cliff. In the distance, it seemed to protrude about four inches. From then on we walked with me close behind Alan, who was testing out the ground - or lack of it.

It wasn't so bad after all. But then, on a bend, the path was non-existent where it had slid down into the roaring waves. Alan skipped across the gap and I followed on to a path of sorts. We realised that the earlier view had been an optical illusion, and although the drop to the right is sheer in places, if we did not suffer any vertigo, then we would not have any problems. We could then enjoy the views, which were fantastic, then at the last bit, a rocky headland featured, like a mini Striding Edge from the English Lake District, but with trees on the top, and a drop down into the Ocean to the right. We finished the walk in good time and caught the bus back to Funchal from a place called Porta da Cruz. Altogether a splendid day - full of surprises. As I said - Madeira is different.

The people of Madeira are a friendly lot, always having time to give directions, if required, and friendly in every way. But one thing that did surprise me was the amount of beggars that we encountered, in Funchal and on the hills even in remote areas. For instance in Funchal, real professionals plied their trade with a certain amount of devotion to duty. When we were there, an old woman would be brought into Funchal, by car, left outside a large store for the day, where she would lie by the side of her begging bowl, then be picked up again at night and taken to her villa in the hills. That's what I call professionalism.

One day, on our day off from walking, Alan and myself had been ambling through the municipal park, the Jardin de Sao Francisco, a place of exotic and exquisite trees and flowers. The park also has much grassy areas where weary trekkers can doss, resting from the previous day's hiking. Alan and I fell asleep on the grass but had our slumbers intruded upon by a man in a distressed condition, with ripped clothing and bare feet, one of which was deformed. He only said one word: 'Escudo.' which he said while holding out his hands.

I woke up in bright sunlight, reached into my pocket, pulled out all the loose change I had, then tipped the coins into the man's eager hands. The man turned, looked at what his hands held, then said: 'More escudos. Not enough.'

Alan sat up rubbing his eyes. 'What?'

'More escudos,' the man's voice had taken on a threatening tone.

Alan then stood up and faced the man, a nose to nose job. 'What?'

'More escudos.'

Alan's voice matched the man's in hostility, and he told the man to go away, but using stronger language. There was also a threat to engage his foot with a certain part of the man's anatomy. The man shrunk away cursing, then from a distance shouted something nasty in Portuguese, before retreating, still cursing. He must have had one pocket without holes in it because he put my change into it. He then shouted a very English swear word from afar, obviously having used it before in the park to people who hadn't coughed up enough escudos.

A night or two later, in a convenient bar, the same beggar entered, but this was not the man we had seen begging in the park. This time the man wore an open necked shirt with a heavy gold chain clinging to his chest. Gold rings adorned his fingers and seventies style flared trousers, not ripped, hugged his hips. Platform shoes hid his previously bare feet. The begging game was thriving in Funchal and we decided never to hand over escudos in the name of charity again.

Other times, in the town and on the hills, we were approached by countless numbers of children holding out little bunches of flowers, sometimes wrapped in Sellotape. These kids were usually not aggressive, and at least they had made an effort to get some escudos from tourists. But once, on the hills, on one of the longer levada walks, we were more or less attacked by an army of children, some thrusting tiny bunches of flowers at us and demanding escudos. And they had a back-up of bigger kids who were aggressive and demanding, and blocking our way on the path. This confrontation was soon resolved when I chucked a handful of change down the hill, sending the Madeiran hordes chasing the scattered coins, and fighting among themselves for the money, which gave us time to escape along the levada path.

But generally we found the walks quiet and rarely met other walkers, although once part way across a narrow ledge, we came across a German couple who were having a problem. The woman was having a severe attack of vertigo and couldn't move. The sheer drop down must have been a thousand feet and it was directly over a road. The ledge was only a couple of feet wide, and the woman had frozen in panic. It reminded me of Barney on Yewbarrow; she did not want to go on, but wouldn't go back either. Our dilemma was getting past her, which made her worse, so we had to help her get back to the start of the ledge by shuffling her feet sideways, inches at a time, which took ages.

The levados go everywhere, and the water flow can be controlled by locks where the canals pass through buildings attended by lock-keepers. The lock-keeper can divert water from one valley to another by very simple means. But the odd thing about levados is that from a distance the water appears to flow upwards. It's obviously an optical illusion caused by the perspective of the scenery, but Alan swears that it's magic. The levados and paths also sometimes pass through tunnels roughly hewn out of the mountains, and following these, torches are required in that blackness - mainly to stop you falling into the water or banging your head on low tunnel ceilings. These are the things that make Madeira different.

We found a small but good restaurant near the market, which was run by two brothers who both looked like Groucho Marx and with the same humour. The brothers were friendly and funny and did a good line in tomato soup in which floated an egg, a meal that became our favourite. During the day that area was alive with market stalls and traders but at night groups of men stood on corners chatting. One night after a day's walking, and the evening's descent from the hotel, Alan and myself were strolling to our favourite restaurant, oblivious of anything but the thoughts of good wine and tomato soup that came with an egg. We were near the market and it was dark. A dog growled from somewhere close and we looked down at two beady eyes glinting in the darkness over a row of bared salivating canine teeth which served as a warning not to get any nearer to the dog's master's front door. Suddenly a voice came from somewhere, offering certain services of the physical kind, and I looked around to see a black hooded shawl that almost covered the face from whence came the voice. The Anglo Saxon wording was unmistakable and to the point, and the offer was repeated.

'What?' said Alan looking round and down at the person of the night who would have benefited from being covered completely.

Broken and blackened teeth smiled between the black curtain. It looked like Marty Feldman in drag after a day of having ugly make-up applied. I think the world's oldest profession then employed the world's oldest women.

'I think she likes you,' I had the nerve to say.

'And your friend with my friend,' said words from under the hood as another version appeared, but much worse. The dog growled and adopted a stance as do dogs when they're about to bite huge chunks of flesh off someone, with quivering lips and squinting eyes.

'I'd rather have the dog,' said Alan, moving on.

'Can be arranged,' came a voice from the crypt.

We moved on. At least they had humour. The cackling from under the hoods was like little puking sounds. I think the dog was laughing too, and holding its stomach, like Muttley.

Later over bowls of tomato soup from which eggs like amazed eyes glared up at us, we told the Marx brothers of our brief encounter of the lurid kind. They laughed, as they mostly did, and said that we should have had the dog, although it would have cost more and we would have had a better time.

On our homeward journey we had the same captain with the perverse sense of humour. Getting ready to take off, the plane backed up as far as it would go before falling off, then it was announced over the Tannoy that a giant elastic band was being attached to the back of the plane and being stretched to its limit. 'You will then encounter G forces upon take off as the plane will be catapulted from the runway, hopefully in the direction of England.' Everybody laughed, but the take off had been described perfectly by the captain.

Looking at the photographs later, of those awesome green pointed peaks, sometimes swathed in Transylvanian type mist, I could imagine Tyrannosaurus Rex crashing through the lower exotic plants, to rip lumps out of grazing plant eating dinosaurs of the placid and boring kind. Madeira, as I have said, is different.

The "Garden in the Atlantic" enticed us back in 1996. Well, it enticed Alan, who was going for two weeks with a group of friends, and when I found out I booked a week to coincide with his first. Luckily our hotels were close together near the coast. On this holiday, we ate out at night mostly in good restaurants but I never once had the famous tomato soup with an egg. The fake beggar was not in evidence, but he was probably by then the owner of one of the upper class restaurants, which he had purchased from all the escudos collected in the park. We didn't do quite as much walking on that trip, but I will never forget one funny episode after a long day's hiking. We had walked down a very steep hill for some hours to find ourselves in a small town from where it was hoped we could catch a bus to Funchal. The streets were amazingly steep and our feet were sore from the long descent. Also our knees had been taking some strain, and we found that on the town streets, we could manipulate the crazy gradient better by walking backwards. I don't know who suggested it but it certainly worked. But some locals from doorways looked agog at the foreigners. It was like Monty Python's Ministry of Silly Walks, with a single file of idiots, all chatting and walking backwards as if that's how walking should be done.

On this trip we hired the services of a mini bus taxi driver who looked after us well. One day took us to the island's third highest peak, Ariero, from which we witnessed some of the most awesome sights ever.

We were above the clouds on a sandstone coloured mountain and in the near distance, more mountains protruded through the pure white blanket, that looked solid enough to bounce up and down on. Our path ahead was well marked and other people thronged around. This was obviously a tourist attraction and not just for walkers. Suddenly we were on a narrow spine flanked on both sides with metal posts holding a handrail over which was a sheer drop down into the clouds. Below the clouds was just guesswork but it must have gone on forever. The spine looked too narrow to be self supportive, more like a path to a fairyland castle in the clouds: not quite real. John and Gail have a pub in the English Lake District, and are well used to getting up hills, but John nearly did a Barney on that spine, when he looked down at the vast drop into nothing. He had to be calmed by us but momentarily looked as if he was going to faint. That day we couldn't carry on as intended because there had been a landslide or something so we had to go back.

Once, I had the day to myself and found on the map a levada that passed near to my hotel. I spent most of the day following the small waterway as it meandered through banana plantations, passing villas with pools and running more or less parallel with the coast. I followed it until a vertiginous drop to the left and some overhead restrictions made it impossible to continue safely. But the views were stunning. Stunning and different, as was everywhere in Madeira.

10   WILD EMPEROR AND WILDER MEN

One place that has been beckoning me back now for some time is Austria. I'd been there as a fourteen year old, with the school., and then again in 1991 with Sylvia and another couple, Frank and Jean. Frank of Mallorca fame. As we were being driven back to the airport by coach, I couldn't help but notice an awesome mountain range, with a dragon's back of knobbly peaks that from the road seemed unclimbable. The long mountain range ran parallel to the road and the ascent through forests seemed close to the road. Looking up through the coach windows, the high rocky cliffs looked vertical and out of reach, as if only by the use of pitons and ropes, or by parachute would one get on to the jagged tops. But then, squinting through bright sunlight, I was sure that I could detect pencil thin trails on those higher parts. They had to be paths, but for flies or Spiderman with suction clamps on his hands and feet.

It was the following year that I read somewhere of the Kaisergebirge and recognised the mountain range immediately. The Emperor's Mountains were the one's I had been in awe of from the coach, and they had many paths, some for the walkers who might want a gentle stroll through forests, and there were those for the more adventurous. The Kaisergebirge is also a heaven for the skilled mountaineer and rock climber. I made up my mind straight away that I was going to the Kaisergebirge.

Taking someone who suffers acute vertigo on the second rung of a ladder to that awesome mountain range might seem a bad decision, but that's what I did. Anyway, Barney was the only one available and at least I'd have a laugh with him. Maybe I could organise some flat walks?

'Of course I'll be OK,' said Barney, as if I'd hurt his dignity. 'I'm a mountain man.'

We had had a little drink at the time, at a family party, in our house.

The delightful Patricia, not one for mincing her words, said, 'I'd better get the policies out, just in case.' Everybody laughed, but Pat.

'If you do fall, can I have your rucksack?' I asked, knowing that I needed a new rucksack.

'The will might be in it,' said Pat. 'Look for it.'

'Patricia, dear, would you miss me?' asked Barney looking hurt.

'Just make sure the paperwork's in order before you go,' returned Pat. 'Or you're not going.'

So Austria it was to be. I sent off for some maps of the Kaisergebirge area and bought a book: Mountain Walking in Austria, by Cecil Davies, which did feature some walks on the mountain range of our choice.

Austria, as I already knew is a country of clean, crisp air, good beer, endless mountains and green valleys from which you expect the Von Trapp family to come skipping out of through fields of edelweiss.

We picked a small hotel that was also a working farm, with a bar that the locals used as their meeting place. The hotel was situated just outside, but within walking distance, of a small village to the south west end of the Kaisergebirge. Nearby was a chair lift to the top of the nearest mountain, and according to the maps, walking paths were everywhere. From the hotel, over some fields, the Wilder Kaiser filled the landscape.

The Kaisergebirge is basically made up of two great spines, the Wilder Kaiser - the Wild Emperor - to the south and the Zahmer Kaiser - the Tame Emperor - to the north. The Wilder Kaiser and the Zahmer Kaiser are joined by a crossbar of hills. To the east of the wilder Kaiser, a lower tree topped ridge with sheer cliffs continues from where the Wilder Kaiser ends; this is the Niederkaiser - the Lower Emperor. Everywhere you looked was a Kaiser of some description. Kaisers were boringly common.

For many miles around, the majestic Wild Emperor dominates the landscape. The knobbly top has many cols and secret dark places, the places that nightmares are made of. Well Barney's nightmares anyway.

I had planned two walks on the Wilder Kaiser, one on the Zahmer Kaiser, and some lesser walks on lower local hills. According to the book, many of the higher walks had the benefit of fixed wire ropes, handrails and metal ladders, all secured into the rocks, as aids for the adventurous mountaineer, and to give the likes of Barney nightmares for life.

We arrived at our hotel in the evening and already the bar was full of local people already well into a good drinking session, and I did detect a sign of over indulgence. The locals greeted us heartily and I knew instantly that we were going to enjoy our holiday because the bar was full of drunks. Later we walked into the village and sussed out the local hostelry.

One thing I have found out in Austria, is that some of the smaller villages and towns shut up shop after the evening meal, and then there's nowhere to go. People disappear as if by magic at night and the places are like ghost towns with bad weather. But our village was not like that, and the handful of bars were well used and friendly, mostly patronised by Germans and Austrians. Most of the local towns are ski resorts in winter and this was no exception. Many ski runs could be seen descending down through clearings in wooded areas.

Nearby was the town of Kufstein, which is on the Munich - Innsbruck motorway, and only just on the Austrian side of the Austrian - German boarder. The walk up the Zahmer Kaiser would begin from Kufstein, a town with an impressive but grim fortress. You could imagine Vlad the Impaler's great grandsons and granddaughters living in Kufstein. Maybe old Vlad himself.

After a few beers in the village, we went back to our hotel and joined the company of locals at the bar who again made us very welcome. The Austrian people, I found, had a very good, but sometimes weird, sense of humour. The Austrians laugh a lot, especially when they've had a lot to drink, and because we did also, we got on very well.

The next day we sussed out the area, did some small walks and bought another map from a local shop. One thing about Austria is how well planned everything is regarding mountain walking. The paths are well marked and the each town has a map of the area: A Wanderkarte - the walker's map, and with the map usually comes a little booklet which relates to the map. All the paths on the map are colour coded to show the degree of difficulty, with a broken line being the path for experience mountaineers only. In the mountains the paths are made obvious by the red and white markings, on trees, rocks or any other suitable surface. A general rule, I found is, if a path has no markings, then it's not the path to take, no matter what, unless you want to go to a vampire's lair. In other words, stick to the marked path. Also, even high up in places that are difficult to reach, new looking signposts are there where paths meet, to guide the walkers. So with the map, the book and the signs, it would be pretty difficult to get lost. Having said that, on my last trip to Austria, our hotel owner told us that many people were killed every week on Austria's mountains. Barney and myself though were mountain men (Barney's words) so we would be all right.

From the local information office we got a bus timetable and found, over the week, that the busses were predictably reliable, with boring old Austrian efficiency.

Along the south side of the Wilder Kaiser mountain is a path, where the wooded areas meet the higher rocky area, and snakes its way along the full length of the mountain. This is called the Wilder Kaiser Steig, on which a walker could; given the time, walk the mountain's length, and even stop overnight in the alpine huts along the way. In fact, with the Wilder Kaiser Steig and the other paths linking the Wilderkaiser with the Zahmer Kaiser, a walker could spend a few weeks on the mountain range without ever having to come off it.

Austria is such a clean and colourful place where every house or hotel balcony sports many flower boxes which are absolutely overpopulated with flowers that look as if they're about to take over the houses or even the villages, like triffids. Barney made the point that the place could do with some good old English graffiti to make us more at home. He was only joking of course, but one day we did see some graffiti on an underpass in Kufstein and it was in English so maybe the Austrians had imported some English vandals to cheer us up.

The first walk we did was up one of the many paths leading to the Wilder Kaiser Steig. The walk up was steep and along a good path leading through wooded areas. Large cow pats at irregular intervals had to be strode over, an act that usually disturbed thousands of flies from their lunch.

'Have you noticed,' asked Barney, as we passed one particularly large pat that could not be seen through its thick covering of hungry flies, 'that some piles of shit attract more flies than others?'

'It has come to my attention,' I responded, knowing that the conversation was about to enter a more profound dimension.

'You see, to me and you,' Barney's face took on the seriousness that the high plane of conversation deserved, 'that is just a pile of shit.'

'But not to the flies,' I added, feeling my way into the mood of the moment, and fighting off the flies with shit on their feet.

'Ah, you've got it,' nodded my friend, as would a professor to a first year student. 'You see that pile of shit is, to the flies, a restaurant.'

'That's where they eat out,' I said.

'Exactly. And that was a five star one, not a table left in the house.'

'There's probably a little fly on the door not letting people in.'

'Oh, they have to book in advance.'

'Austrian efficiency,' I noted.

'That one was an Egon Ronay recommended restaurant, as advertised.' Barney was getting into full flight.

As we passed more cow pats, all complete with dining winged masses, we gave each pat a grade number depending on the number of flies at feast. Some were only two star and at one, flies had to bring their own wine. Then an old pat, dried out in the Austrian sun, looking crisp and ready to crumble, did not have one fly in attendance.

'Closed by the authorities,' said Barney as we strode over the dead, fly-less faeces. 'There'd been a lot of complaints about the food.'

I nodded knowingly, and we marched on to higher places and hopefully a higher level of conversation. Later, through the trees, the rocky heights could be seen above, eventually dominating the view. Then we were on the Wilder Kaiser Steig, the main path of the mountain, and the views were awesome, above and below. Above, at close hand, the rocky tops loomed over like giants. The most westerly top, Scheffauer to our left, overlooked the town of Kufstein as if it was the town's keeper. Down and across the valley, villages were too small to recognise. To our right much snow was gripped in the cols and pockets below the higher Wilder Kaiser peaks. Above higher, grey clouds gathered over the grim peaks adding that certain foreboding that mountains get in bad weather.

We sat down by the side of the path and ate our sandwiches while enjoying the view. This is what I'd come to Austria for. I knew instantly that I'd be back to climb higher one day. We were not on a ledge yet Barney was not happy looking down at those unrecognisable villages. But looking up was worse. Getting back was Barney's priority. He had gone a funny colour which I remembered from years ago on Yewbarrow.

Getting back, the easy path eventually dipped, leading across a stretch of sloping scree that had patches of snow clinging to the loose stones. The path ran across and slightly downhill, towards a heavily wooded area at the other end of the scree. Barney was quiet but fine until getting to that first stretch of snow, the remains of a heavier winter carpet. Maybe he thought that he was going to slip down, and it wasn't the place to get vertigo. Downhill, fir trees were everywhere like a green rug. His legs became jelly and swearing bounced off the screes as would yodels. Getting across that scree, and snow, was a toil but the relief at entering the woods was obvious as those small stones were no more. I was every curse imaginable but Barney had done it. We marched on, the jelly leaving his legs, and some humour returned to our conversation. We were heading for the small town of Scheffau but still had some way to go. Eventually a couple, German, came towards us. They greeted us in German, then realising our nationality, spoke in English.

'Have you had a good day?' asked the man, smiling.

'Have I had a good day?' snapped Barney. The Germans grew worried by my friend's expression. 'This person is trying to kill me.' He didn't say person but used very foul language to describe me.

The couple looked alarmed, bade us farewell and carried on, unsure, towards the scree. We headed down towards Scheffau. Eventually the town's rooftops could be seen between the trees, which made Barney happy. The bus would not be far away, then he would be happier still.

That night Barney told anyone who would listen, that I'd tried to kill him.

The next day was one that I was dreading, because we had planned to go up the local mountain by means of the chair lift at the back of our hotel. I was to be surprised.

We were late, and approaching the chair lift, found ourselves in the midst of twenty or so young German men who were all laughing and shouting on the grassy slope.

Getting to the top had to be done in two stages and one of the lifts - or maybe both - was one that transports people in single file, scooping you up like in a giant spoon, and then taking you up to the mountain top, over the grassy slopes and high fir trees. I can't remember if it was the first or the second lift, but which ever it was, when we reached it Barney stopped in his tracks at the site of people being scooped up like dollops of ice cream that were then transported skywards.

'You won't get me on that,' said Barney, shaking his head.

The young Germans were having a great time, now they were arguing with the man who operated the chair lift. Some had bottles of beer for the trip up. Teutonic spirits were high as Austrian beer was being consumed, and the chair lift man was getting more agitated.

Then one of the young men was climbing on the chair lift, shouting excitedly while those on the ground chucked ale down their throats like it was going out of fashion. The Von Trapp family would not be amused, especially as some German youths urinated on to the grass. Some urinated, some drank beer, some did both.

Suddenly Barney amazed me: 'If this lot can do it, then so can I,' he said with determination.

I was first on, with Barney behind. Ten beer swilling youths were to our front and ten were behind. They rocked the hanging seats for fun and the chair lift man was furious. They were all shouting and so smothered the shouts by Barney as we all sailed skywards. I looked round to see Barney cringing in front of a beautiful backdrop of the Wilder Kaiser mountain on which I could just make out the whiteness of that problematic scree, between the rocky top and the lower trees, that had given Barney so much trouble. His face was a frozen statue, his eyes not moving. Vertigo had taken over.

Eventually his frozen lips melted enough for him to shout; 'I don't like this,' as the ground grew further away.

Youths behind him were shouting and laughing, as were those in front of me. Every one, but Barney, was having a great time. Barney swore louder into space.

Eventually, after one last surge upwards, the ground below levelled out, and a man stood ready to help people off the chair lift. The youths in front were falling all over the place and the attendant wished he had not turned up for work. I was helped off then I watched as Barney's wide eyed, frightened face loomed nearer. When his feet landed on *terra firma,* the relief was evident but composing himself took some time. The young men headed for the bar of the restaurant that graced the mountain top. We looked for the path to take us further and away from the rowdy crowd, on a journey that Barney had no problems with. Barney has always been a stronger walker than me and soon was striding away on the good path without any steep drops to its sides. All the horizons were mountain tops and we walked for most of the day, before returning to the chair lifts to take us down again. As we passed the restaurant great frivolity was being enacted by a certain group of Germans, who we chose to ignore. We descended to our hotel, which was worse than going up for Barney.

That evening during our meal, a noise could be heard through the hotel walls. It sounded like a thousand people were having a good time wrecking something. It was twenty young German men who had been drinking since at least ten o'clock that morning. It was then about eight o'clock in the evening. Now they were finishing off in the beer garden of our hotel, a path we had to take to get out to the town.

Later, Barney led the way, while I cowered in the doorway. My friend had to push his way through a sea of waving arms, much spilt beer and a deafening roar of slurred German words, which we wouldn't have understood, even if they hadn't been slurred. Then the lads confronted Barney, pulling at his anorak and joking as if he could understand them. They wanted to be his pal or kill him. Some stood up and put arms around him. What they said, I will never know. Then two of them had their noses but inches from Barney's. The mood looked grim, but I think heights frighten him more.

'Shut it.' Barney can shout quite loud when he wants and his words out-volumed German partying.

The following silence was if someone had flicked a switch. Two drunken youths stared into Barney's face through watery eyes. One of them said something in his native tongue.

'I'm English,' explained Barney.

'Englander,' slurred a young voice. Some of them laughed into their glasses. 'Englander, mmm.'

'That's right, Englander,' said Barney. 'And I bet that at least one of you speaks good English.'

'Quite correct,' said one of them. 'I shpeak perfectly good English.' A young man of about twenty-one, looked up from a table. He looked as if he was about to collapse.

'And I can see that you lads have been having a good time, and I don't blame you.' Barney slapped the English speaking drunk on the back. 'You carry on, lads.'

The English speaker explained something in German and all the drunks wanted to shake Barney's hand. 'Where are you from?' asked the interpreter.

'Manchester,' replied Barney.

'Manchester United,' came the drunken reply from many.

'We are from Munich,' said the interpreter.

'Good footballing town,' added Barney.

The interpreter said something and they all applauded. I then ventured out among the drunks. 'This is my mate,' said Barney, and they all wanted to shake my hand.

'What's the occasion?' asked Barney.

'Who needs an occasion?' replied the interpreter.. 'Actually somebody is getting married next week, but I can't remember who.' The interpreter laughed and explained his joke to the others who fell about laughing.

'Have a good night,' said Barney, pushing out through the crowd and making way for me. I escaped while I could.

Much later, after Barney and myself had found a corner table outside a village bar, and consumed two or four beers, from the previously quite village street, the drunken hoards could be heard before they could be seen. Then a police car, cruising at the speed of the drunks, appeared. Young men were falling all over the place, then as they neared, from across the street; 'Hey Englander.' The young men waved at us and we waved back.

'We have lost one,' shouted the interpreter. 'Have you seen him?'

'No,' we shouted back. A policeman got out of his car, and looked over at us. Then the policeman spoke to us in German, to which our reply was a blank stare. The policeman neared menacingly.

'English,' explained Barney, as the officer of the law was at the pavement on our side of the road.

'Are you with these people?' asked the fuzz, without any sign that he had ever smiled.

'Never seen them before,' said Barney, turning from the officer, who glared for a few seconds then about turned, wondering what on earth two middle aged Englishmen would be doing with twenty inebriated young Germans.

'Manchester United,' shouted a drunken German accent from afar. 'Goodnight English friend,' shouted another.

The worse for wear lads then began slogging up a road that led presumably to their hotel. Some ten minute later, the missing one appeared, and was so drunk he could hardly walk, repeatedly falling on to the pavement. From afar a policeman watched until the drunk followed the footsteps of his mates.

'That's what you call having a good night,' said Barney, before catching the eye of a passing waiter.

The next day we caught a bus to Kufstein, near the German border, and from where the walk up the Zahmer Kaiser began. It was while we were heading for the start of the walk, that again Barney commented on the boring cleanliness of everything. Then out of the blue - there it was - some graffiti on this wall, and in English: a few swear words and then MUFC.

'Doesn't it make you feel so much better?' asked Barney, nearly crying with gratitude. 'Somebody is thinking of us after all, making us feel at home.'

Thankfully that was the only graffiti we encountered during our time in Austria, and Barney said he would come back and visit the writing on the wall if he ever got homesick.

We eventually found the start of the walk, which turned out to be a steep, but obviously well used path. Many walkers were grouped along the path. As we got higher the north side of the Wilder Kaiser made itself evident, looking totally different to the south side that could be seen from our hotel. In a way this side was more beautiful, or at least had 'an away from it all' picture, probably because there was no sign of roads to link it with civilisation.

'I wonder if my Patricia has found the will,' mentioned Barney, as we walked side by side.

'You haven't fallen yet,' I assured him.

'I nearly did the other day on that scree.'

'Rubbish - safe as houses.'

'But I would have chucked you my rucksack, on my way down,'

'Thanks. Then I'd have had to phone Pat to tell her, that I had saved the rucksack.'

'That's what I call a good pal. Tell me - how would you word it?'

'I'd say: Patricia, I've got some good news and some bad news. The good news is I've got his rucksack, but the bad news is Barney is..'

'Call me Bernard,' interrupted my pal. 'If I snuff it, she'd like that.'

'Okay: Bernard is ... brown bread.'

'She'd understand that,' said Barney. 'Brown bread - don't mince your words.'

'And then she would say; 'Is the will in the rucksack?'

Barney looked at me as we walked. 'You know my Patricia well.'

'And then she would have gone off the line looking for the policies.'

'She'd probably contest the rucksack, knowing her,' added Barney.

Ahead, sounds of the human kind could be heard, laughter amid many voices, and a building came into view, by the side of the path. We glanced at each other, both thinking it could be twenty young German drunks.

Suddenly some very large brown cow pats lay on the path, steaming in their newness. They were so newly delivered that they were devoid of flies who had not got the word yet. The large animals who had made the deposits sat idly by.

'New restaurants open up every day round here,' commented Barney. 'And they've not had time to advertise yet.'

'The food's fresh,' I added.

'Organic,' said he, being pedantic.

'Exactly,' I agreed, stepping over a large steaming brown mound. A giant brown and white cow looked on with great disinterested eyes, twitching an ear to unsettle a nuisance fly that should have been on it's steaming deposit.

The building was a large hut complete with beer garden in which a couple of dozen people were sitting at tables, and being served food and beer by two waiters. The people all waved to us as we passed, and Barney commented that we would call for a beer on the way back. Some people shouted in German and gesticulated. I think they were telling us to forget the walking and join them for beer. But we walked on over fly-less cow pats, ignoring the invitation.

We were heading towards a mountain called the Pyramidenspitze, although we knew that we'd have to turn back at a certain time in order to get the last bus back from Kufstein. We walked until eventually reaching a grassy mound where we sat and ate our lunch. The north side of the Wilder Kaiser was a splendid sight and its upper rocky parts changed colour from a slate grey to a deep purple as large white clouds massed overhead, muffling the suns rays. Looking down, a carpet of fir trees lined the valley. Looking down, Barney decided he'd had enough. A sign pointed right towards the Pyramidenspitze. After lunch, we turned back towards Kufstein where we were just in time for the last bus. On our way down the same people were still drinking in the beer garden and this time we accepted their invitation to rest over a beer or two.

On the last night in Austria, we decided to have a good booze up, which started in the town and finished up in the hotel. Friends we had made joined us and we drank into the early hours. I do not remember going to bed, but when the alarm clock went off in the morning, Barney looked over at me from his bed and called me a bastard for getting him drunk. It was all my fault of course and on the coach he moaned all the way to Innsbruck Airport, once nearly stopping the coach to be sick. At the airport we both felt worse and were dreading the flight home which was a couple of hours late. Outside it was raining heavily but we sauntered out on to the airport grounds and stood under the rainstorm getting soaked but feeling better. Two concerned airport policemen came over to us, obviously thinking we were escaped lunatics, and asked what we were doing outside in the rain, but when we told them it was to cure a hangover, they just laughed and walked away, telling us that we were crazy, which we knew anyway. All the way home Barney called me all the uncomplimentary names at his disposal and has never let me forget that I was responsible for his hangover from hell.

The year after the hangover from hell, Barney agreed to accompany me again to Austria, on the condition that I wouldn't get him drunk. He said that in the presence of My Patricia, who interrupted with: 'Don't blame him, it's your fault, stupid.' Very knowing is Patricia. 'And don't take him on any steep hills,' she added, looking at me.

That second time with Barney was just as hilarious. We stayed at another hotel cum working farm, this time, just outside Kirchdorf, a small village to the east of the Wilder Kaiser, the opposite end of the mountain to where we stayed the year before. Most of the other guests were from the area that had been East Germany before the Berlin wall had come down.

On our first night in the hotel, we sat in the lounge watching a football match, surrounded by the Germans, who we soon got into conversation with. The young father of one family explained that it was his first holiday outside Germany which was only possible because of the uniting of the two Germanies. Barney felt sorry for the family and when it was time to pay for the drinks, Barney insisted on paying for the German family's drinks. The family shook our hands and went off to bed leaving Barney smilingly satisfied with his charity. The next day, after breakfast, as we were leaving for our walk, the German family were heading off to somewhere in there brand new BMW car. They waved as the gleaming vehicle purred over the hotel path towards the road. 'They should have bought us a bloody drink,' moaned Barney as the car disappeared from view. 'That's what happens for being a kind person. But I sleep well at nights.'

Barney's vertigo caught up with him on a path up to the Niederkaiser, that long ridge that overlooks the road joining St. Johann with Kufstein. From the road, the white cliffs appear to rise vertically and are topped with a fine green line of trees. The path on top is the Wilder Kaiser Steig, which continues along the Wilder Kaiser and carries on to the other end of the mountain, to where Barney had the problem with the screes the year before.

From the area known as Litzfelden, one and a half kilometres south of Kirchdorf, we had to climb up the hillside to the Lourdsgrotte (Lord's Grotto) a shrine cut out of the rock face, then carry on the ridge path to where the Wilder Kaiser started. The route took us between houses and farms and eventually a sign indicated the Lourdsgrotte, up through the woods. As usual the way was marked with red and white paint on anything paintable, and the path got steeper as we climbed. Barney was having no problem with the ascent and strode on ahead of me. Then after a while, the path could only be taken by using the wire rope handrails that were fixed to the rock faces for support. Timber ladders and stair treads aided our climb as the going got steeper but amazingly Barney coped with all of this without a problem. Then we were at the grotto, where a cut out in the rock face houses a small Madonna statue and some candles that are sometimes lit by local people. On the other side of the path, the ground drops steeply into dense trees. Barney had shown no fear up till then, until two young women appeared and stood with their heels over the steep drop so they could get their cameras focused on the shrine.

'Oh, don't stand there, love,' warned Barney to the girls who knew no English. 'You'll fall.' Barney moved towards the startled girls, his arms waving frantically. 'Come away from that ledge.'

The girls stared at the waving foreigner as if he was a mad, demented troll, then continued to focus their cameras. Come to think of it he looked like a mad demented troll.

'Hey, love, move. Oh dear...!' Barney had gone into vertigo mode, this time on behalf of someone else.

The girls had had enough and shooed Barney away with some hostile German vocabulary that can only be guessed at, and carried on taking pictures. Then, photographs completed, they gave Barney a distasteful look, and carried on up the mountain.

Barney leant against the rock face for support and shook his head. 'That's me finished for the day,' he said. 'I can't go on. Jesus, I though they were going to fall.'

Well I wasn't going to miss out on this walk so I carried on, leaving Barney to get himself back down to Litzlfelden, from where he could walk along the road to Kirchdorf, frightening people on the way with his troll impersonation.

I carried on up the steep path until I reached the ridge from where I had a marvellous view down into the valley. Below me the white cliffs were a sheer fall into the woods. Probably Barney was better off turning back where he did, because in parts the path was only a couple of feet from the edge. I laughed at the possible headline in the Tyrol Daily Sport: 'English Troll Stalks Hikers on the Neiderkaiser. Women not Safe.'

The walk was a great success, at times using fixed ropes and ladders to navigate the steep parts, and the path at times was perilously close to the unprotected sheer drop. The views were tremendous, especially towards the end of the Neiderkaiser, looking up to the most easterly peak of the Wilder Kaiser, the Maukspitze. Then under the shadow of the Maukspitze, I turned north to head back down some easy paths, through woods, then fields and eventually to Kirchdorf, where I expected the locals to be hunting down a crazed troll.

Our next walk was up the Kitzbuheler Horn, the mountain local to Kitzbuhel, the famous ski resort. We started the walk from St. Johann, and this was Barney's forte, with absolutely no steep drops to the sides of the paths, and it was me having trouble trying to keep up with my pal, who strode up effortlessly like a mountain goat. We had a beer at the top then caught the cable car down again, and a bus back to Kirchdorf.

Another walk that year, a very easy one, was a long hike where we eventually got caught up with some aged German hikers, about twenty or so, with a couple of guides. This was another walk where Barney was in his element and was striding away from me. As we were heading downhill through a densely wooded area, the path was riddled with the roots of trees. It began raining heavily causing the mud on the tree roots to become very slimy underfoot. We were then in the middle of the group of Germans who didn't seem prepared for the wet weather, and all opened umbrellas to combat the rain. We couldn't believe it, but with one hand in the air, clutching at umbrellas that blew about under the heavy wind, most of them slipped on the muddy roots. They looked like a load of aged Mary Poppins characters but flying about without control. We spent ages dragging the Mary

Poppins impersonators to their feet, and tried to tell them to put away their umbrellas, but to no avail. We gave up in the end and left the group to slip and slide to their hearts content under the foul conditions. The guides seemed clueless about the situation. Barney called the guides some very unpleasant names, but then we marched on, undeterred.

I was at Barney's son Paul's wedding in Sheffield, when, at the dinner table, I mentioned that I had nobody to go abroad hiking with that year. 'I'll come with you,' said a voice close by. The owner of the voice was a slim, bearded guy who's eyes beamed at the thought of going to Austria for a week of hiking. I had consumed a lot of beer at the time and thought nothing of it, thinking the bearded man was allowing drink to do the talking for him. But when he turned up at our house the next day, I realised his intentions were true.

This was Jim, who lived close to me, and a keen cyclist who had cycled all over Europe and was obviously as fit as a butcher's dog. After showing Jim the maps and the pictures from my previous trips to Austria, he was hooked.

We went to Ellmau, a small town on the main road, central to the Wilder Kaiser, and looking up to the Ellmaur Tor (The Door of Ellmau) an enormous scree covered col between two of the Wilder Kaiser's peaks.

Jim turned out to be one of the fittest people I've ever walked with, in spite of him being a few years older than me. On the front of my guide book is a stunning photograph taken from the Ellmaur Tor, looking down the snow covered scree, to the valley far below, with white capped peaks in the distance. To the side of the scree, enormous grey cliffs reach up to jagged tops where trolls might party, but not Barney the Troll.

From the photograph, it looks like a sheer drop down to Ellmau. Barney would have kittens just looking at the photograph.

On our second day in Austria, Jim and myself climbed up to Ellmaur Tor, on an amazingly steep path to the side of that awesome scree. Fit Jim raced ahead like a mountain goat, and I had to keep shouting to him to wait for me. The view got more stunning as we climbed up, and as we got higher, the temperature dropped considerably. Not many walkers ventured to the top, and when we reached that fantastic col, only a handful of walkers were there. The photograph on the front of my guide book is a terrific picture but it does not do justice to the place in reality. There was still a small carpet of snow huddled among the screes, and the view across the valley was marred by some cloud, but this only added to the atmosphere, and the sheer cliffs rose up to disappear into the clouds. I think many trolls looked down at us, laughing, from secret places. The view to the other side - to the north - was just as splendid, and walkers came up the path, as if from nowhere, and the drop down back to Ellmau looked far too steep to get back by. I began to have great sympathy with Barney as a sudden dizziness threatened to control me, but I fought it by sitting down on the rocky ground to eat my sandwiches.

Getting back down was more of a trial because we could see the drop down at all times, but it was good to pass those hikers sweating buckets and breathing heavily on the way up. The highest point of the col is 1997 metres above sea level. That night we had to sup great quantities of beer to replace all the fluid we'd lost. That's one of the plusses of going to Austria, the good beer, and a lot cheaper than Iceland.

I think we went on a small walk the next day but the day after that we had planned to get to the top of Scheffau, the most westerly peak of the Wilder Kaiser, named after the town of Scheffau which nestles on the lower southern slopes of the Wilder Kaiser. From below, Scheffau looks unclimbable without the use of an escalator, and I did have my doubts about us succeeding to the top, although I had read somewhere that it could be done. All the cliffs appeared sheer, but looking closely, through binoculars, a faint excuse of a path could be seen snaking upwards, but it was as if only flies could manage it unaided.

We caught the bus to Scheffau and started the walk. I can't remember which of the paths we took but which ever it was, Jim the mountain goat, strode on and upwards through woods and fields towards the Wilder Kaiser Steig, that great high mountain path from which all other higher paths break off at various intervals. Memories of Barney the year before came flooding back as the higher we climbed, the more familiar the scenery became. Then as we neared the main path, those awesome summits loomed overhead and to the east, the Wilder Kaiser Steig snaked along under troll's lairs. There was no stopping Jim, but I had the map, and I had to frequently call for him to wait. On those higher places, it was not done to go off course. I remember a vertiginous ledge on which we had to wait for some people who were stuck there, doing a Barney impersonation, being dizzy and clinging to the rock face. But it was an excellent walk with thick wire ropes fixed to the steepest faces, just to add to the adventure. On the summit, the view was tremendous, with, to the west, the River Inn weaving through the valley to as far as the eye could see. To the east, the mighty ridge of the Hackenkopfe joined up with the Elmauer Halt peak at 2344 metres from sea level. Our summit, Scheffauer, was at 2111 metres but it seemed much more. Somewhere, over to the north was Germany. It was definitely troll country, and being a clear, sunny day, much of Austria's panorama could be seen in its splendour. Also it was a first for me, being the only Wilder Kaiser peak that I had reached. We took many photographs then sat on the grass and unwrapped our sandwiches. From below it is hard to believe that there is grass on the top, an unexpected bit of greenery, on which to place our rucksacks. Then, as though the rustling of sandwich paper was a signal, a half dozen enormous black birds joined us for lunch. The great winged monsters must have done all this before, because they waited patiently gawping with their beady black eyes as the sandwiches were unwrapped, then stepped forward, beak first. Now I think that these feathered fiends had put a spell on us, because neither Jim nor myself could eat the sandwiches, no matter how hard we tried. In fact they tasted foul, the sandwiches not the birds, if you excuse the pun. We put it down to rushing up the mountain in the heat, We both said that our stomach muscles ached, and only the drinking of our bottled water satisfied our culinary desires. The birds ate every morsel of our cheese and ham butties, then looked at us questioningly, then menacingly when the table was bare. We took this as the point to leave the mountain top, especially as more flying monsters were circling overhead. I think a troll, looking amazingly like Alfred Hitchcock, peeped from behind a rock, as I packed up.

The way down looked frightening. That fixed roped seemed to dangle into nothing but endless space, but it was the only way to go and I didn't want to stay there with The Birds. As I clung to the rope, with my feet groping for a foothold or two, I knew that those birds were watching, and probably laughing, knowing that they could fly, and I couldn't.

The way down was steep, vertiginous and exciting, and we eventually reached the scree that had hated Barney the year before. I think his swearing still lingered on, faintly whispering in ghostly tones around the rocks. Funnily enough, I found the scree very hard going this time, something I hadn't noticed the previous year - probably because then I had Barney to worry about.

Back in Scheffau, we just missed the last bus back to Ellmau, so we decided to walk, an absolutely catastrophic blunder. My stomach muscles were aching and I needed a drink as if it was going out of fashion. Also the deadline for dinner was nearing. What seemed many hours later, we passed our dining room, with minutes to go. Jim nipped in to tell the waitress that we wouldn't be long changing, but when we did return, showered and dressed for the occasion, neither of us could eat anything. We ordered beer to go with our meal but that's all we downed, then more beer, then more. We put it all down to dehydration after all the effort of the day under the burning sun, probably having walked for ten hours in total, which seemed twenty, including that last endless bit on the road. That night we had lots of beer but, honestly it was purely for medicinal reasons.

The next day we rested, just going for a gentle stroll somewhere on grassy parts. My stomach still ached, and I felt out of sorts, so I decided to go for a swim in the hotel swimming pool, while Jim had a sleep. Coming out of the swimming pool, I noticed a door leading to the health spa, in which there were saunas and other healthy activities for the weary walker. The notice on the door had me pausing momentarily. It was directed at English speaking people, pointing out that, once through the door, bare skin was the order of the day, the wearing of clothes forbidden. Really needing a sauna to soothe my stomach cramps, I went in, but hesitantly, to firstly enter a changing room, where clothes had to be removed. A large man, naked but for spectacles, greeted me in German. I nodded, noting the overhang of his stomach that was being used to conceal his manhood. His equally naked wife was his clone, and I wondered which was the man.

Naked, but for my waterproof watch, and clutching a towel, I entered the inner sanctum. It was like bellies-r-us, at first. I have never seen so many large people. I sauntered to a sauna and entered. A couple, twentyish, sat chatting. They weren't fat. I nodded and sat down next to them, sweating buckets in the heat. Eventually it was all too much for me, and I could have supped Ellmau dry. I think I suffered a mild panic attack in that confined space and with all that heat, so I got out and headed for the showers, dripping sweat all the way. White bodies were everywhere and in the showers people of both sexes stood under the hot jets. I showered off the sweat, then enjoyed the cooler water before getting out feeling refreshed.

I was sitting on a form, leaning over to pull up my socks when a voice, near to, spoke in German. An albino beaver was but inches from my nose. The German furry animal engaged me in conversation to which I could not reply.

'Ich bin Englander.' I explained.' Sprechan zie English? I had never spoken to an albino beaver before. Well, not in German anyway.

'Sorry,' said a voice. And I realised that the fluffy lump was attached to the pubic area of a tall slim blonde woman in her twenties with the figure of an athlete and breasts that pointed horizontally over my head towards the wall as if a spirit level had been used in their design. The acoustics of the place caused the woman's voice to be thrown downwards. 'It is very hot in here.'

I agreed wholeheartedly, and dried off the sweat that had started to seep from me in rivers, before escaping to the cooler parts of the hotel. The woman was still throwing her voice as I bade her farewell.

'Auf Wiedersehen,' said the beaver.

'Auf Wiedersehen, pet,' I replied.

It's now time to introduce my good mate Tommy Greenwood, who was brought up in the back streets of Manchester's Newton Heath. Tom served with the British Army in Aden and Malaya, as part of the Desert Mountain Rescue Team working on airfield construction. He was probably the reason why the hostilities went on for so long and I think peace was guaranteed if Tom was removed from both of these places. So you see, Tom was instrumental, but unsung in the scheme of things. Becoming a joiner in civilian life, Tom, being the parent part of a one parent family, a job in itself, studied to obtain a degree in Construction Management, and is now employed as a building site manager, whilst still studying to better himself even further. But he doesn't get any better, he gets much worse.

There is a downside to this, being that Tommy and Barney are mates, but I don't hold that against either of them. We all have a cross to bear, and they are each other's. They both are also mine. Barney and Tommy do go hiking together, an unlikely liaison, and I have been known to make it a threesome, but you can have enough of a bad thing. We were like the Three Stooges, all we needed were hammers to hit each other's noses with. Shep, Larry and Mo, scurrying over the peat bogs of Kinder, arguing about which was the correct path. Barney wanting the path without a drop to the side, Tommy charging through high ferns, covered in camouflage paint and screaming obscenities while waving a large curved knife, and me getting them all lost with a broken compass. I can remember once, somewhere high up over Ladybower Reservoir, when an obscene mist had engulfed the planet. Three streams met at one point, so that there were three lumps of land, all separated by water, and each of us was on one of those lumps of land. Mad cascading water at the bottom of ravines like rambling Grande Canyons, separated us, and yet we were together only seconds earlier. This was a plot by the evil mist so that aliens could get us singularly. Tom shouted for Barney and myself to join him on his blob of land, and Barney did the same to Tom and myself, both insisting that he was right. But I was right, not them, and I did have the map. I think it took about two hours before we joined up on a common course of action, vowing never to go hiking with the other two again.

We were having a party once at our house, with Tom not being invited. The thing about Tom is that you do not invite him, because he likes to gatecrash. Anyway, about just after midnight, Tom turned up with his dog, Teddy. Tom had been taking Teddy a walk, when he just happened to see the merrymaking through the window, so he thought he would call, bringing Teddy into the fun.

Now Teddy at the time was well past his sell-by-date, and being taken for a walk was a trial by both dog and master. The house was full to the brim and young and old were swaying to the melodious and loud music of ABBA. Somebody, feeling sorry for the dog, who had settled on the carpet between the dancers, gave Teddy a sausage, and somebody else, who will never be invited to one of my parties again, gave Tommy a pint of Boddington's bitter.

Then, as sexy Swedish voices were well into the chorus of Waterloo, Teddy threw up the sausage, and the contents of his last six meals, all over the carpet with the velocity of a fireman's hosepipe. One of the dancers, a sister-in-law of my youngest daughter Karen, was well into pregnancy, and seeing the animal's impression of a fire hydrant, ran to the door throwing up into her hands. She caught most of it, hurling it into our front garden, but then others copied her, covering my lawn in multicoloured spray.

Tommy, meanwhile, thought the whole thing was hilarious, then laughing uncontrollably, poured the cream of Manchester down the back of our couch.

Sylvia, a cleanliness freak with zero tolerance for bad smells, went berserk, and it took until the early hours to clean up the mess. That was Teddy's Waterloo.

Thankfully, Teddy was put down not long after that night, but really it should have been Tom, who has threatened to get another dog, if it could come with a guarantee to destroy people's parties.

Tom decided to come to Austria with me, and we went there in 1998. At Manchester Airport, Tom informed me he was having a problem with his bowels, and on the plane made a number of speedy runs to the loo which was a few thousand feet away, and probably on another plane. Manchester to Salzburg is approximately two hours, Tom was in the plane's toilet for three. I think Teddy had passed on some chronic bowel problem to its master as a joke legacy from the grave.

We had picked the old town of Kitzbuhel to stay for our week, a place I had been to once for the day, probably with Barney. Kitzbuhel really has got everything, including its own mountain, the Kitzbuheler Horn, the top of which can be reached by cable car, or by walking. We walked. The town centre is not unlike a Spanish resort but without the sea, with tables and chairs set out for the visitors, outside the many bars. It even has a casino. In summer, in good weather, the place is alive, and sometimes it's impossible to get a seat in the centre. Our hotel was Austrian *Olde Worlde*, with everything made out of wood, including the owner (only joking Franz) Austrians use wood like everybody else uses plastic. I think there was wood in the breakfast too. Being an ex joiner, Tommy loved all that wood, and we spent many boring hours critically examining the roof constructions of countless buildings, bridges and wall panelling. But the hotel front door opened directly into the town centre where it was all happening including a plague of wasps which were threatening to close down the town. We thought that the wasp was the town emblem, because every bar seemed to own a few million.

I had four possible walks organised, the first we started by going up a cable car directly from the town, at the back of a bus station. This cable car is a great silent experience, gliding up over the greenery towards the mountain top where a restaurant serves food and beer. I had my back to the ascent, looking at the marvellous views of the Wilder Kaiser looming behind Tommy. Now I knew that Tommy did not have any vertigo problems so when he began to bite his lip and push his knees together, I wondered what his problem was.

'I've got to go, pal,' he said as the cable car was probably two thirds of the way up.

'Go where,' I asked, knowing that there was nowhere to go, whatever he wanted. The cable car was very high over the ground..

'Need a toilet, pal. And now.' Tommy began to stand up in that confined place.

'You have to be joking,' I said, seriously thinking he was.

'It's no joke, pal.' Tommy had a sort of pleading and straining look on his face. He clutched at the window, fumbling. 'How do you open this?' he growled.

Now, it doesn't take much imagination to know that any Austrian Health and Safety Executive would not give its blessing to openable windows in cable cars, especially when carrying people from Sweden, with their history on suicide.

'It's not meant to,' I said.

However, a small widow high up did open, marginally, by sliding.

'Here you are,' said Tommy, fumbling with the belt on his trousers.

'Tom,' I yelled. 'You just cannot do it.'

'They bombed us in the war, now I can bomb them,' he said falling back on to the seat. 'Have you got a polythene bag?'

'Not the Austrians,' I said. 'Anyway, we're nearly there.' The top of the hill could be seen nearing.

Then with a mighty last push, we were there. Tommy dived out of the car and ran to the restaurant faster than I have ever seen him move. He reappeared smiling broadly, as if he'd just won first prize in a knobbly knees contest.

'Sorry about that,' he grinned, 'but when one has to go...'

We marched on, along what was aptly signposted as the Panoramaweg, a beautiful trail through trees, with a splendid panoramic view to the right of the mountains. We were joined by the total able-bodied population of the German speaking world and a handful of British tourists. The Panoramaweg was like Piccadilly on a Saturday but a thousand times more crowded. We fought our way into the route march, and headed the way everybody was going, not using our feet but being carried by the crowd. As the Panoramaweg ended so did the crowds, who turned back on a return path. It looked like a human carrousel ten people thick. Part way along this overpopulated trail, Tommy had to go back to the restaurant for obvious reasons, but how he fought back through the masses had me bewildered.

When he returned we carried on, eventually finding ourselves in quieter territory, behind us the crowds thronged. Ahead, the path meandered along a ridge which we followed. Later, we returned to the cable car and much of the route marching was over. We glided down in quiet comfort without any further attack of the runs, and sauntered back to the town centre for a beer or two just before dinner. There had been more people on the mountain than in the town and the town was crowded. We each had a giant ice cream before the beer and were joined by a hundred wasp families including children who wanted ice cream - ours. When the beer came, a few wasps lined up on the rim of the glass to practice diving. I've never seen a wasp perform a triple backwards somersault with half twist so perfectly. The waiter applauded and gave the wasp a full six for artistic merit. Even the froth wasn't disturbed as it entered the beer, but the wasp could not swim and it drowned, watched by its stupid friends who followed it into the beer but without the same style.

The next day it was the Kitzbuheler Horn, the town's own mountain, the one Barney and I had been up. And we had planned to walk up by a tarmac path, not realising that most people went up this way by motorised vehicles. It was a hard slog up that route, but we joked as usual all the way up, and Tommy congratulated himself for his bowel's lack of temperament. But then it happened, near to the top, just before a sharp bend in the road.

'Gotta go, pal,' said my friend, vaulting over a fence that was there to stop people from falling off the mountain. I cringed and peered over the fence to see Tommy on a rocky ledge not far down, mooning to anybody below. 'I'm all right,'

Relieved that Tommy hadn't fallen to his death, I relaxed and lay on the grass beside the road. It was a hot sunny day and I thanked Tommy's bowel activities for allowing me to sunbathe. My legs were weary after the long uphill walk, so it was good to relax for a while.

'All right?' I shouted.

'Wonderful,' came the strained reply.

I didn't know the coach was coming until the last second, as its wheels made crunching sounds on loose stones. It had come from the mountain top, turned a bend, and there it was trying to defy gravity by using a low gear and brakes. But its passengers had seen me because they were waving; elderly people, with any hair that they had being snow white. I waved back, smiling, thinking that we should have used a coach to get up the mountain. Then I realised they were not waving at me, they were waving to a point somewhere over my head. Suddenly there aged expressions changed, some were laughing, some put hand over eyes, some pointed.

On the ledge, Tommy waved back from a stooped position as his shirt end fluttered in a breeze, not allowing being sociable to interfere with the business at hand, which was being delivered to some place a few hundred metres below.

The waving tourists disappeared down the hill with something to discuss over the next few days, and five minute later Tommy climbed over the fence smiling with satisfaction.

'Friendly bunch,' he remarked. 'Come on, chop, chop, let's go.'

I struggled to my feet, struggling because I was crying laughter.

'Is something funny?' asked Tommy, threading his arms under his rucksack straps. It was five minutes later when a smile etched across his face then he had to stop because his laughter made his stomach do impersonations of a jelly with a vibrator.. 'Told you I'd bomb the bastards, didn't I' All the way back in the cable car, Tommy had a wry smile on his sunburnt face.

Later, before dinner, we ordered giant ice creams in the town centre, at a place that seemed devoid of wasps, but was full of tourists. But when the ice creams came, a black cloud appeared over the town centre, heading in our direction. It was the Kitzbuhel and District wasp diving club, that eventually settled on our table waiting for the beer to come.

The next walk was to be the biggy. I had already climbed to the top of the most westerly of the Wilder Kaiser's peaks, the Scheffauer, now I fancied the Maukspitze, the most easterly peak. It appears from wherever you view this peak that the only way up is by helicopter, but guide books told me differently. And this was to be a three day affair, with us having to stop at one of the mountain huts before and after the final ascent. Making enquiries in the town we managed to get a key for, what we were told was an un-manned hut just below the final ascent up the rocks. So we stocked up with food - cooking facilities were available - and drink - red wine and some beer, and made our way by taxi from the town. The woman taxi driver took us part way up the mountain to a point where further progress was thwarted by road works, so we had to walk from there.

First we had to aim for the Wasserfall (waterfall) which was well sign-posted and reached by a good path that wandered through wooded areas, quite steeply. We hadn't been going long, when I took a wrong turn which led us to someone's house.

'Oops,' I said, realising my mistake.

'Do you know what you're doing,?' questioned Tommy, snatching at the map which I held firmly. 'You'd better let me navigate from now on, if you're going to get us lost.'

'We're not lost,' I argued, pulling the map from Tom's grasp, 'just temporarily diverted.'

'Give me that map. You're useless,' growled Tommy, diving for the Wanderkarte that I hung on to.

He eventually got a hold on to the map, but I held firm, and we both fell to the ground, struggling as four passing hikers stopped to watch the wrestling match.

'Give me that map,' ordered Tommy, but inserting swear words between that and map. His body was under mine at the time, so I put a booted foot on his chest and wrenched the map from him.

The four hikers looked at each other in alarm and moved quickly away from the affray. They had never seen violence on the mountains before. Well not since the Second World War. Maybe they thought this was the start of the third.

'Help me', shouted Tommy from under my boot to the retreating hikers who were not going to look back.. He told them I was a word that probably did not have a German equivalent. The hikers pace increased. Maybe it did.

I soon found the correct path, on which we followed to the Wasserfall with Tommy moaning all the way about not getting any help from strangers, when needed. The waterfall itself was a bit of a let-down when we eventually got there. I had expected a great foaming sheet of vertical water, like a mini Niagara, but this one turned out to be a fine spray like rain. But the setting was awesome, with the spray cascading down a sheer rock face, as is someone was holding a finely holed watering can at the top.

We settled there, in the company of a young German couple, to have lunch. With the German's broken English and my multi-fractured German, we had a conversation of sorts. The Germans were not going much higher, just through the woods, then were coming back down on another path. I told them that we were stopping in a hut for the night, then tomorrow it was up the Maukspitze. The Germans looked at each other, making expressions and noises that one could relate to horror movies when the victim is confronted with the silhouette of a monster through the kitchen window. I wondered if I had explained properly.

'What do they know that we don't?' questioned Tommy.

We moved on, but minutes later, and a bit higher, Tommy let out a squeal of joy, and began pointing.

'Look. Austrians are wonderful. They've built this just for me.'

Against the rock face was a little wooden building with a corrugated roof and a heart shape cut out on the door.

'Ein sheissen hausen, und just for little old me,' explained Tommy.

'Word's got around,' I said. 'Probably by someone who was picnicking below the Kitzbuheler Horn, yesterday.'

'Bloody efficient buggers, these Austrians.' was all Tommy could say.

'Well, are you going to use it?' I enquired.

'Don't need to, pal,' he said. 'But the thought's there. And look at the woodwork. See that little heart. That's the Austrian way of saying with love to Tommy.'

'To stop you crapping over cliff edges,' I added.

'They're quick to learn,' noted my friend. 'Come on.'

Eventually, we found ourselves in a high plateau, with the Maukspitze looming ahead. There definitely did not seem a way up its sheer sides. The weather was clear so that all the easterly peaks were obvious. Trolls and other horrible monsters must have been watching us from hidden lairs, licking their lips with purple veined tongues. Also, I bet that devil-birds with bibs on were perched around a table cloth covered summit. Maybe that's what the Germans knew about the Maukspitze.

A building high up to the left, looked inaccessible, but there were no others, so we climbed up a steep trail to it. Clambering on to where the ground levelled out we could see that it was indeed the hut - and with people.

One man lay on a form, sunbathing, and another sat on the step drinking beer. A blackboard leant against the gabled front wall, advertising the price of beer and food. And we were told it was unmanned.

'Gutten tag,' greeted the beer drinking one.

'Ich bin Englander.' I explained.

'Well, hello, there,' he said in perfect English.

The one on the form turned his head slightly, then struggled to a sitting position to greet us. 'A beer, perhaps?'

'No, I'd like two,' said Tommy who was sweating profusely from that latest effort on the ascent.

The shirtless man disappeared into the hut and returned with two bottles of beer that were ice cold.

The man on the step asked us where we were going and when we said that we were stopping at the hut he looked amazed.

'You have got the key from the town?' asked the other.

'Yes,' I said.

'I will show you to your room later,' said the shirtless one, 'but for now, rest with your beer.'

Tom said it was the best suggestion of the day, so we sat on the grass with the amber nectar that must surely have come out of a fridge. Later it was explained to us that a solar panel was fixed on to the roof. A solitary wasp lurking in the grass waited for us to settle, then set off for town to tell his mates that we had arrived.

We were then asked if we'd like to join the others for a meal which would be served in about half an hour's time, an invitation we couldn't refuse, so we didn't. The shirtless man then took us to a side door which he pointed to: 'Your rooms, gentlemen.'

The door opened into a kitchen complete with table, chairs, a cooker and a sink. From the kitchen a ladder took us up to the sleeping area, an unbelievably large dormitory with many floor level beds covered in something reminiscent of wire wool. But this was now home and as they say: home is where the heart is. Outside, a miniature hut was a toilet, built, I think, over a precipitous drop. It reminded me of a similar experience in Iceland. It would be like Tommy on the Kitzbuheler Horn, the day before, but being covered in. Tommy considered it wonderful and rushed in to use it.

'They think of everything,' he beamed, coming out a few pounds lighter.

Later, after a rest on the wire wool, we entered the dining room to eat. The shirtless man was now dressed, and he, it turned out was the host. We'll call him Hans. The other was a German Hiker from Stuttgart, who was doing a five week solitary walk around the Wilder Kaiser area. They must have long holidays in Stuttgart, or where-ever. We'll call him Edmund.

'Would you like some red wine?' asked Hans, plonking a bottle on the table. Tommy and myself nodded like nodding dogs that smiled. The glasses weren't wine glasses but this was not the Casa Belmondo in Royton. 'Hang on,' I said going before back to the wire wool room and then returning with my bottle of red wine which I plonked on the table.

I think the meal was chilli-con-carne - I remember that it was spicy - and it was much better than anything I might have served up in our new kitchen.

Edmund offered a toast dedicated to Austrian -German- English unity to which we all touched glasses over the chilli-con-carne. I felt a little uneasy, especially at the wry smile that was beginning to appear on Tommy's face.

'I'll drink to that,' said Tommy.

We all drank to the toast, then Edmund asked if we had anything worth toasting.

'To the mountains,' I suggested.

'To the mountains,' echoed the others. We drank.

Edmund said something that was the German equivalent of cheers. Something like 'Bombs away.'

'And to the friendship of mountain climbers.' said Hans, shyly.

Cheers.

Bombs away.

We drank the wine, then got stuck into the spicy meal. I hoped there would be no more toasting, noting that Tommy had the expression of somebody who was about to giggle.

The meal tasted wonderful, but I suddenly missed the wasps, and I hoped that they could make it in time. It was getting dark outside, and the sound of rain could be heard battering the roof. Then the dull boom of thunder shook the hut like an earthquake. With our plates clinically empty, Hans scraped out the remains of the meal from the pan, distributing the chilli evenly. We all had exactly the same numbers of rice grains as if he had counted them.

'That was superb,' said Tommy, as our plates shone with their emptiness, to which we all agreed.

Then the wine had gone. Where had it gone, it was there minutes earlier? But I then realised where it had gone, because I was feeling the effects.

'What's for dessert?' asked Tommy, patting his stomach appreciatively.

'I only have beer,' said Hans, looking hurt.

'Oh, go on, then.' said Tommy. 'I don't mind.'

Hans went to the fridge and pulled out four bottles of beer which he brought to the table. We poured the stuff into the glasses, replacing the wine. They looked more like beer glasses anyway.

I can remember feeling a little drunk as the evening went on, and the conversation deteriorating with the usual decay of articulation associated with drunks. We were laughing loudly about something absurd when there was frantic knocking on the door. Trolls, I thought, or the wasps. Hans got to his feet, wondering like we all were, who on earth could be on the mountain at this time of night, and in such weather. It could only be trolls, I concluded, fearing the worst. Or wasps, or The Birds.

It wasn't any of these things. It was worse, Italians. Italian women to be precise. About five of them, and completely lost, and wet through. Hans couldn't speak Italian, so Edmund, who could, went to the door. When he returned, he said that he had asked them in, but they looked frightened and refused. They said that they'd shelter under the canopy until the rain stopped, then move on down to wherever.

We thought it very strange to be wandering about at that high level, so late at night. Edmund said it was Tommy's laughing that had frightened them off and I believed him.

How we got talking about the war, I can't remember, but I'm sure Tommy started it. Hans looked decidedly uncomfortable and moved his chair backwards nearer the wall.

We agreed on one thing, which was that British and German humour was pretty much alike, and Tommy said that we should never have gone to war with each other, to which Edmund wholeheartedly agreed. We were quite drunk at this point. Then Tommy suggested that Germany and Britain should have got together and bombed France. Tommy kicked my leg under the table and we waited for a response.

'Splendid idea,' said Edmund.

Hans had got further against the wall, wishing he could get through it, not realising it was a wind up. Tommy went on with more wind ups and Edmund joined in. Later, we staggered out into the freezing night air, looking into the surrounding blackness and feeling the rain that blew in all directions. We could have been blown off the mountain but we did not realise it until the next day.

I could have slept on a clothes line, so the wire wool gave me no problems, until about four o'clock in the morning, when thunder disturbed my slumbers. I awoke sweating cobs in that insulated upper room that was like a furnace.

'Have we started a war?' shouted Tommy from his wire wool cot, as a clap of thunder exploded to be closely followed by lightening that momentarily filled a window with streaky light. It was like being in a ghost train without moving.

By the time we stumbled out to meet the high level Austrian morning, the thunder had died down, but a thick mist hid most of what was higher than us, like the Maukspitze where we were supposed to be going. Looking down it was obvious that Austria and probably the rest of the world had disappeared under grey mists that looked like smoke.

'There has been a war,' said Tommy. But below, the mists were moving, and some land shapes were beginning to show through.

Edmund, who had been sleeping on the veranda in a sleeping bag, appeared with a worried look. 'I think the Maukspitze is out of the question, gentlemen. Or any other mountain top for that matter.'

'You haven't slept outdoors all night?' asked Tommy.

'Yes, smiled Edmund. 'I was warm enough, but the thunder was a problem.'

'Those women didn't come back?' I asked.

'Well, yes. That's why I was so warm,' said Edmund. He looked as though he meant it. I wondered.

We waited for about an hour or so before making the decision to cancel the climb up the Maukspitze. The mist clung thickly to all above us and did not give any sign that it was about to shift. There weren't even vague silhouettes of mountains through the gloom and climbing up would have been impossible, so we began the trek down, disappointed at out failure. It was bad enough going down, but at least the mist on the decent was patchy, with visibility enough to see the red and white paint marks on the trees. Oh, well, there would be another day.

Later from Kitzbuhel, the Moukspitze and all the Wilder Kaiser peaks were still hiding behind that damn mist. From our hotel balcony we could just make out the plateau under the hut, but everything above that was a blur. I vowed to come back one day to climb that elusive peak.

The next morning we stood on our balcony staring with disbelief at the mountains. The sun was shining, the sky was blue and the Wilder

Kaiser was so clearly defined that every crevice, crag and col could be seen clearly. Tommy even reckoned that he could make out the hut with aid of my binoculars. We swore at our bad luck but laughed at our experience in the hut, grateful that we hadn't started a war. Edmund was still up there, somewhere, among those awesome peaks with the trolls who must have had a great time in the mist the night before. Maybe Edmund was a troll.

On our last night we said a tearful farewell to the wasps, and I tagged along as Tommy paid homage to everything made of wood, which was everything. On the coach to the airport I stared at the Moukspitze peak, hoping that one day I would return, and helped with good weather, get to the top.

11   MILLENNIUM MAD COWS

According to some pundits, the world was going to end with the start of the Millennium, but it didn't, although now in November as I write this, many of Britain's main streets are submerged under the murky waters where our rivers have overflowed their banks after the torrential rain from hell that has been unleashed upon us, the worst for hundreds of years. Maybe the pundits were right after all, and it is happening, but slowly. Mind you, what might be devastation for some, has been an absolutely wonderful experience for others, like the swans I saw on television gliding gracefully down the river which days before had been a street somewhere in Yorkshire, oblivious to the humans being rescued by the emergency services nearby in rubber dinghies and other floating crafts. But not to make light of the matter because this flooding has caused so much heartache with some families losing everything for the second time around. All I'm saying is that for the swans it was fun, a sort of holiday.

Tommy and I didn't book our holiday early just in case the world did end, therefore saving any money we might have laid out for nothing. Just being cautious, that's all. Another reason for not booking early was the fact that Tom's working pattern was a bit erratic, with him never knowing when one contract would end and another begin. Also I was busy with my work, and to synchronise our leisure time got worse as the year evolved.

I nearly organised a solo trip somewhere but gave that up because I don't think I could stand my own company for a full week and anyway it would not be as much fun. Also I might get killed, falling down a precipitous drop in some dark corner of Europe, never to be found, and maybe eaten by wolves, or wasps. At least if I did it with Tom, or Barney, they'd get a laugh out of it, although Barney might get a bit dizzy seeing me plummet down into nothing.

Early on in the year I called in at Pole Travel, the local travel agents who had organised most of my holidays over the past fifteen years at least, and had to fight my way though the crowd of would be holiday makers who obviously didn't think that the world was about to end, just yet. Jean, helpful as ever, was on hand to offer me obscure names of faraway places with mountains, where pots of beer could be purchased for about two pence, and heavenly hiking paths would take me up to breathtaking heights, but never mentioning murderous gangs, lurking in caves, that kidnapped people and cut off their bits to send to the authorities in order to obtain a ransom. Ever full of advice is Jean, as are her staff, who are blessed with the greatest of patience when dealing with indecisive people like me. 'How about the Macha Picchu by yak? All right then, we have a five day fell run up to Thabana Ntlenyana? No. Seventeen week backpacking with Attila over the Steppes of... No? God you're hard to please. Seventeen pub strolls from the *Cat And Fiddle*?'

'What have you got in Spain?' I'd been thinking about Spain for a while. Anywhere near the Picos De Europa? Not quite as wimpish as the Cat And Fiddle. Jean brought in help and soon the shelves were being scoured for accommodation in Northern Spain, to culminate with a pile of brochures being dumped on her desk. The pile resembled a breeze block in thickness, but heavier.

'There you are, northern Spain.' The Pole Travel staff looked pleased, but then, thinking that I might change my destination, dived out of the way to answer imaginary telephones, leaving me to haul away this mountain of papers on my own.

Tom had suggested getting a ferry to Santanda on Spain's northern coast, then driving to the Picos where we should - his words - find accommodation in different locations as we move on. But the date that he was available also coincided with the Spanish national school holidays, which, as enquiries were made, meant that every bed in the Picos was booked up for that time. I was told by one authority that it is difficult to even park your car in the Picos area during the Spanish holidays, when people park up and picnic just yards from their cars. It sounded like around the Derwent Reservoir at Easter, when the real hikers can't get near the place for picnickers. I hate Easter at Derwent. In fact I hate Easter in most places.

Then Tom changed his availability, or had it changed for him by his employer, then changed it again, then again. Then it happened: he was free. A date had been fixed for the completion of a project.

'Book it,' he demanded. 'Anywhere.'

I booked Austria, again; and Kitzbuhel again; and the same hotel, again. Well we didn't have much time, and even then there were not many rooms that remained available in the whole of Kitzbuhel.

It was September of the millennium year that we were eventually going to Austria. Tom's brother-in-law drove us to terminal two at Manchester Airport that Saturday morning. Part way there I enquired, quietly as to the condition of Tom's bowels.

'Perfect, pal,' whispered Tom with a wink. 'In tip-top condition.' He patted the pronounced bulk of his stomach and smiled with the satisfaction of a healthy person. His gut looked bigger than on our last visit to Austria. But I just knew that he was fit.

I knew that he was in reasonable shape because we had been on some training hikes over the previous month. One was a trek over William Clough from Hayfield, then up on to the Pennine Way, up to Kinder Downfall and back down past Kinder Low, and back to Hayfield. We did this at a fast pace and without problems, so then I suggested Striding Edge, which Tom had never done, but had always wanted to.

It was a Sunday and the sun was shining as we left Failsworth, with Tom driving. Turning off the M6 at junction 40 the sun was still shining and then driving along by the side of Ullswater we realised that we must have picked one of the best Sundays of the year. Patterdale, as usual, thronged with hikers, and we just caught the last parking spot on the car park. The way up to the start of Striding Edge is easy to find and soon we were off the road heading upwards. The sky was blue and in front and behind, hikers toiled enthusiastically with one aim; the Edge. Tom trailed somewhat but never faltered as we aimed for the start of Striding Edge. On the actual edge Tom had no trouble at all and coped with all the tricky bits without a problem.

Tom had brought telescopic aluminium walking sticks which had been given to him by Barney. I had given them to Barney after buying them in Austria some years earlier and never really taking to them. We noticed one particular group of people that kept passing us, then we would pass them, about eight strong, of all ages.

Then it happened, about half way across the Edge, dark grey clouds had come overhead as if by magic, then enormous hailstones like marbles crashed down on us, hurting our faces. Activities on Striding Edge ceased immediately as people sought shelter where there was none, hugging the rocks and turning their faces from the ice bombs. Then just as swiftly it stopped, but overhead got darker and Striding Edge had become a different place, one of danger as children clung to parents as their feet slid over the now slimy rocks. We plodded on, then just before the final ascent it happened again, but this time much worse. When we finally got on to Helvellyn top it had stopped but we were soaked and cold. Tommy plodded on, digging those sticks into the ground. The sun peeped through grey clouds, and that group of people passed us - or was it us passing them. We carried on, then finding the path down which passes Red Tarn, on which we were in the middle of that other group. Pleasantries were passed between us but then Tom and I stopped to let them regroup to our front. Later, I was some way in front of Tom and caught up with the group who had stopped for a break.

'Where's your mate?' enquired one of them.

I looked back and could see Tom navigating a tricky step down, prodding the ground with his sticks as would a blind man. 'Oh he's all right,' I said. I can see him. Actually he does well being nearly totally blind.' Tommy prodded the ground from where we had descended. The group looked upwards.

'Good heavens,' said a woman, 'Look. He is blind.'

'Cobblers,' said a man, 'he's having you on.'

Tom prodded the ground as we spoke.

'He is,' said a youth, 'he's got a white stick.'

'Two actually,' I corrected.

'Good heavens,' said someone.

The man looked at me as would Chris Tarrant when someone gives an answer to the half million pound question on Who Wants To Be A Millionaire, when he asks: 'Final answer?'

But the group moved on down hill while I waited for Tom. When he caught up I explained; 'The people in front think that you're blind.'

'I felt it up there,' he responded. 'Where are they?'

Ten minutes later, we encountered the group who had stopped to consult a map and were in heated debate about which path to take. I walked by the side of Tom who waved a stick in front of him, testing the ground as do blind people. The group looked on until we passed, some with pity, the man with that Chris Tarrant look still etched on his face.

'Can I stop it now?' asked Tom some time later when the group were too far away to our rear.

'Yes,' I said.

'Amazing what us blind folks can do,' said Tom, charging down the hill, happy.

Kitzbuhel looked as welcoming as ever, and the hotel Manager's wife recognised us immediately. After the usual booking-in procedure she gave us the bad news.

'I am afraid that for tonight you have a room with a French bed.'

We looked at each other. 'What's a French bed?' Tom asked.

'I think you call it a double bed,' explained our hostess.

We looked at each other again. 'No way,' said I.

'It's only for tonight,' said the woman. 'Tomorrow, we'll move you, if you want.'

'We want,' said I. Tom looked hurt.

We lugged our stuff up to our room with the French bed, then toddled down to the front door which opened into the town centre. Kitzbuhel here we are, again. The place hadn't changed, but just to check, we did a tour around the centre. Tom saw some woodwork that he'd missed the last time, and spent some time being in awe of the local carpenters. Eventually we sat down at one of the pavement cafes to the most heart warming events that brought tears to our eyes. The wasps remembered us, and to prove it they were in such a hurry to greet us that they trampled over themselves in the rush, their little black and yellow bodies piling up on some spilt beer on the table top. If this wasn't an official greeting, then I don't know what is. Tom squashed about thirty with a beer mat, a sacrificial part of the ceremony of course. Anyway, we were back as if we had never been away.

That night I slept in the same bed as Tom, right on the edge of it to be truthful, as far away as possible from my overly hairy friend who slept in fits and grunts. In the morning our host, Franz, asked how I went on with my new wife. I replied that my wife is not so hairy, and that I wouldn't be coming back unless I had a bed to myself. Franz laughed but our luggage was moved that day to a room with twin beds.

The next day, a Sunday, we got the cable car up to Hahnenkamm, the mountain that Kitzbuhel separates from the Kitzbuheler Horn. This was the cable car in which Tom had suffered with severe diarrhoea on our last trip to Kitzbuhel, but this time, although watched for tell-tale signs of a dodgy tummy, Tom's bowel problem was conspicuous by its absence. This was the mountain with the Panoramaweg on which the whole of the German-speaking people, two years previous, had been on a continual route march. They were still there, and not even tired after all this time. We pushed our way through the marchers and carried on south along a path that took us over a ridge with fine views to both sides. Again, as ever, the Wilder Kaiser looks down at us, to our rear. To our front, a rocky spine dominates, this is the Kleiner Rettenstein at 2,217m. To our left, the Grosse Rettenstein is bigger and more brooding at 2,362m. In between the two Retensteins a magnificent valley opens up, pointing to snow covered peaks in the distance

. Our aim is a peak named Schwarzkogel at 2030m (6,660 ft) which separates us from the Kleiner Rettenstein, and as we eventually climb the last grassy ascent to the cross on the top, we are the only ones around. The sky is boringly all pastel blue and we are tired after a long walk. As we sit down on the grass to eat and drink, a young man appears from nowhere. The young man is moving fast, almost running but his breathing is easy as if none of what he is doing is an effort.

The young man was wearing baggy white trousers that reached a couple of inches below his knees, a white tee shirt, a hat that John Wayne might have worn on some ranch or other, and solid looking training shoes. There was no sign of a pack. I felt positively overdressed, and definitely out of condition.

The young man stopped, smiled and said something in German. I explained that we were English, to which he nodded and pulled down the tinted shades which hung on his chest by a cord around his neck. He was a friendly soul and spoke rapidly, pointing to distant peaks, then waiting as if I had to answer him. I nodded which seemed to please him and he rambled on, pointing out other peaks to which I nodded every time. I hadn't a clue what he was saying but he was happy with the nods, and I was happy if he was happy. The man rattled on, pointing and there were a lot of peaks to point at.

Tom had a brainwave and asked the young man to take our photograph on the peak which shut the man up momentarily, but he was a perfectionist and had us posing for ages in a variety of positions before clicking. This was indeed a fabulous spot to relax and have lunch. To the north, the full length of the Wilder Kaiser could be seen in all its glory, and to the south, distant snow covered peaks filled the horizon. But we had to get on as we still had some ground to cover, aiming for a place called Aschau which nestled in a valley to the west and appeared as about a half dozen buildings on the map. There had to be a bus stop there. Aschau was connected by road to Kirchberg, which was connected by road to Kitzbuhel.

A woman, in her later forties, had appeared out of the blue and was chatting to the pleasant young man, which was our cue to remove ourselves from this wonderful place. We shouted to our young friend, waved, then turned back down the descent to a path which according to the map, led eventually to Aschau. Soon the young man was passing us in great strides, as if time mattered, but we found our path and headed down hill to the half dozen buildings that were hiding behind the greenery of trees in the valley that looked a long way down.

The path was steep and at some time on this descent, I realised that Tom was having a problem with his knees or at least with one knee. I knew this by the grimaces he was pulling with each step down, and the occasional expletive that rippled through the mountain air.

And then there were the cows. Mad cows, may I add.

Now Tommy, I have to say, is a fearless sort of guy, and mentally strong in the way that not many things seem to bother him. We had slowed down considerably because of his troubled knee, but he wasn't really complaining. All of a sudden, though, I could sense that something was wrong, but could not put a finger on it. The going was not too difficult, but there was a definite crunching of Tom's brow as we made our way along the path which was huddled close to bushes which formed a side to a field. In the field, cows munched grass and flicked at flies with their tails. Every time the cows moved, great brass bells around their necks sounded, to tell you that they were moving.

'Do we have to go through this field?' asked Tom, flinching each time the bells tolled.

'It's the only way down?' I responded. I looked at the map to be sure. 'Why?'

'Those fucking bulls, they don't like me.'

'They're cows,' I said, looking for signs of udders below the great beasts. 'Yep, they're cows.'

'No they're not.'

146

'They are bloody cows, and docile ones at that.'

I moved on, and Tom had picked up speed, in spite of his bad knee. The path led through an opening in some dense trees in a far corner of the field, and when we got there, Tom showed obvious signs of relief, by blowing hard and smiling. The crunched brow flattened as we entered the woods.

The woods cut out the sunlight as I picked up speed. I eventually saw light at the end of the woods for which I aimed, but as I neared the light, the light dimmed. It dimmed because something had moved into it, blocking out the light. It was a cow, or so I thought until nearing the creature which just stood there staring into the woods. The creature regarded me with disinterested brown eyes as I approached, but then did I detect just the glimmer of interest as the animal's eyes seemed to pick up on me? I moved to one side of the path of the animal, searching for signs of hanging udders but found none, just a tuft of hair. I searched again, and on finding udders, I would have shouted thanks for the mammaries, had it not been too corny. But the animal was totally devoid of mammaries because it was a male of the species. A bull, but only a young one, young but gigantic. The bull watched me as I moved to its side and its head swivelled a bit to follow me with its eyes. I thought that the bull's head was going to swivel fully but bulls are not built like owls so it turned to stare again into the woods, and the approaching Tommy, who could be heard crunching twigs with his boots not far away. I was now into the field, under the pastel blue, out of that darkness in which my pal was trudging towards a half tonne of prime beef. I could imagine the bull's ears twitching every time a twig snapped, its eyes peering into the darkness searching out the source of the noise. But it was only a young bull, nothing like that monster in Mallorca.

In the open field more bulls grazed, about eight of the beasts, all young and inexperienced. I searched out hanging mammaries but there were none to be seen, so I carried on along the path, an act which the bulls barely noticed. One or two did look up from grazing, but returned quickly to their munching, bored by the sight of hikers.

Young bulls or not, I did not look back, but moved quickly to the stile at the far corner of the field. I then looked back, from behind the stile. Tom was nowhere to be seen, but the rear end of that young bull was sticking out of the trees at the other end of the field. In the field other bulls were now standing on the path, oblivious of its existence. Then, four or five women hikers marched across the field, avoiding the path and the bulls, heading towards me.

'Your friend has gone around the woods,' said one of the women in a heavy German accent.

After the woman had moved quickly past me and out of sight into more woods, I searched out the field for sightings of my pal, but the only living things were the grazing bulls. Eventually, after what seemed a very long time, Tom appeared from the left of the trees at the far end. He was cautiously creeping along the fence, almost hugging it.

Those bulls, I reckoned, were so used to seeing people on the path that they take it all in their stride, but when the unexpected happens, like someone walking across the field by other means, it takes them by surprise. All the bulls ceased grazing as one, and turned to look at Tommy, curiosity taking over their tiny bovine minds. Then they moved, although slowly, very slowly, but nevertheless moved - in the direction of Tommy. Tommy, meanwhile, was well aware of the bull's interest in him and had reached a state of frozen animation against the perimeter fence. Then Tommy moved and quickly, but so did one of the bulls who began to cantor towards my pal who shouted something, the meaning of which got lost in the breeze.

'Distract the bastards,' filtered across the field as the bull picked up speed, and Tommy clawed at the fence.

I wondered what shoo was in German but shouted it in English, hoping. The bull obviously did not understand English and the cantor became a gallop. The other bulls followed their leader as some animals do.

Tommy was now climbing the fence which was hard up to a dense matting of conifer trees which surrounded the field, then he was over it, clawing his way through the branches, as he'd been trained to do in Malaya, but this time he was minus a panga. The bulls stopped to gaze at frantic Tommy who eventually fought his way around the fence to the stile which took ages.

'So they're cows, are they?' asked Tommy, red faced and sweating, and using expletives between every two words, as he climbed the stile. 'Come on, chop, chop, let's be on our way.'

Aschau was more than a half dozen buildings but only just. We had been walking for about nine hours - we'd have done it in seven if Tom's knee hadn't been a problem - and it was deserted. One of the first buildings we encountered was a restaurant and bar where we ordered two beers which were downed in a millisecond, then asked our host to order a taxi back to Kitzbuhel because we'd missed the last bus by ten minutes.

It was while we were waiting for the taxi, that a woman entered the beer garden. She had been the one talking to the young man on the top earlier, and she gave us a wave as if we were old friends. We waved back, then Tommy engaged her in conversation, learning that she had not come down the fields but had used tarmac paths to get down to Aschau, a fact that Tommy used to vent his anger out on me.

'I knew there was another way down, to avoid those bulls.'

'Not as scenic,' I said, 'or as funny.'

The next day we had planned to go up the Kitzbuheler Horn by cable car, which is done in two journeys. The first cable car is reached by crossing the railway track to the north of the town. To get on this cable car you have to buy a card that you insert into a slot at the turnstile. These turnstiles are mounted vertically with three aluminium prongs which turn as you enter, therefore allowing one person in at a time. We paid, got the card, inserted it into the slot and entered the platform at the lower end of the cable car carrousel where it slows down to allow you to get on. As we were walking the short way to the cable car, Tom had turned to look back then fell on the floor clutching his ample stomach which I think had lost an inch or two on its girth after the previous day's long walk. Tom was laughing hysterically, but as I dragged him to his feet, I noticed a woman hunched up on the floor, clutching her crotch with both hands. I pushed Tom, who was crying laughter, on to the cable car, then as the car picked up speed and the door slid shut, he explained, fitting words between laughs, what had happened. It appeared that the woman had inserted her card in the slot, then somehow stood back quickly, but the turnstile prong had carried on upwards and belted her one under the crotch, an act that sent her to the floor with tears to her eyes, and to Tommy's eyes for that matter.

'You're sick, you,' I said trying not to giggle as the ground beneath us grew further away.

'I'm sorry, pal,' said Tommy. 'Maybe it's my sense of humour, but I thought it very funny.' Tommy collapsed on the cable car seat in a quivering heap of laughter, which made me laugh uncontrollably.

It was a warm day but the blue sky kept mingling with a white haze of misty clouds, as we climbed on to the second cable car, a gondola, I think they call it. This car has room for about twenty people and the operator wouldn't allow it to move until it was full. The car then lurches out and upwards towards the Kitzbuheler Horn's Summit. Tommy giggled all the way. Looking out of the window was like looking out of the window of a low flying aircraft.

'Sorry, pal - it's just my sense of humour,' he kept saying.

A woman nearby, trying not to look down, clutching her husband's arm in a vicelike grip, looked as if she was ready to cry - obviously in fear of heights - wondered what on earth Tommy was finding so funny. Suddenly Tommy bursts out laughing.

'Sorry pal - sorry pal.'

In the corner of the gondola, a woman rubs her crotch for comfort.

Tommy notices this and turns to lean his head against the window which draws laughter tears down the glass.

The gondola lurched upwards then swayed dramatically over a massive drop.

The woman, clutching her husband, goes green and thinks that there's a drunk on board, or an idiot.

'You're sick,' I said.

'Sorry, pal.'

We had planned to walk south east along a path for a few hours then drop down and back into Kitzbuhel. The walking was fairly easy but Tommy's knee was not so good and he struggled to keep up. As most of the walk was on flattish ground - the test would be on the way down, which wouldn't be friendly to his knee - or anybody's knee for that matter. We eventually had to make a descent to - of all things - a dairy farm - but the field was only full of animals with udders. I heard Tommy groan at the sight of all those beasts , and he looked for other ways to get down, which he found - by skirting the field and wading through a deep stream, adding a half hour to our journey. Then we were on a tarmac path leading into town. It had got hotter and we were sweating because we were moving fast as Kitzbuhel could be seen getting nearer. Soon we were heading through a Golfplatz, a nine-hole golf course on the edge of Kitzbuhel, a pleasant path with forms every now and then - where people sat reading books or watching the golfers. We picked up speed knowing that the town was not far away, sweating under the effort. Tommy was limping but fast as if his limp was a natural thing.

'I'm going to get the biggest ice cream in Kitzbuhel,' he mentioned as the town buildings grew nearer. 'God I could murder an ice cream - and a pint of cold beer.'

We staggered through familiar streets to the centre, where Tommy reminded me of that film: Ice Cold In Alex. 'This is Ice Cold in Kitzbuhel,' he gasped, collapsing into a chair outside a street cafe. When the waiter came, we pointed to the heaviest looking mass of ice cream on the menu, which looked like the Kitzbuheler Horn in winter. 'Und zwie grosse bier,' Tommy added as the wasps massed overhead.

That night, after dinner, we had a very lot to drink, having got involved in the company of a German man and his Dutch wife who were there with two children and the man's mother. In fact that night everybody wanted to be our friend and we all started to toast various things and chucked schnapps down our necks as if they were going out of fashion. Then the host came out and because we'd spent so much there, brought out more schnapps and there was more toasting - and more schnapps. And this was after a lot of good Austrian beer and a bottle of wine with our meal. I had been keeping a diary of events on this trip, but do not recall when or how we got to bed that night.

The hangover the next day was nine out of ten for effort. At breakfast, Tom, who's face told the story of the evening before, mentioned to two retired ladies from Kent that he was a lap dancer in a Manchester night club which catered for the more genteel of middle aged lady night clubbers. He asked them if they brought an iron and if so would they kindly iron his leopard-skin posing pouch. They declined his request outright by staring into their muesli and shaking their heads.

On the Tuesday we went by bus to St Johann which is just up the road from Kitzbuhel. This was a day off from hiking and we spent it looking round the town, culminating on a tour of wooden things - such as a bridge over a river. The bridge was a masterpiece of joinery skill, explained Tommy who examined every mortise, tenon and splice, and wondered at the solid beams, trusses and purlins.

On the Wednesday we caught the bus to Kirchdorf, where Barney and I had stayed some years earlier, and we did the Niederkaiser walk, the one where Barney got his Vertigo at the Lords Grotto. Tommy did this with ease with his knee making a miraculous recovery. Maybe the Lords Grotto had an influence in this? Anyway Tom almost skipped up the steep bits, enjoying the fixed ladders and handrails, and wondering at the magnificent view over the sheer cliffs. He reckoned this walk, not the longest of our holiday, was certainly the best for variety and interest and not what he had expected. At one point, sitting on a red painted form - all forms on the Tyrol seemed to be painted red - enjoying the view and having our lunch, a man and woman appeared from the direction we had come. They were German, middle aged and surprised to find two Englishmen sitting there as if time mattered not. The woman spoke excellent English and explained that she had lived and worked many years in England, and how good it was for us to be enjoying the Austrian mountains, because there was nothing like this in Britain. I did mention the Lake District, the Scottish Highlands and Snowdon but she wrinkled her nose at the very thought. She said something about me not being serious and that those places were nothing compared to anything in Austria, but it was nice to meet us and they had to be going because they had much walking to do. They hoped we had a good day and then set off in the direction that we would eventually be going. Now I know that Austria has some spectacular scenery, and much higher than anything back home, and all that, but I wouldn't put down our British mountain areas. Chris Bonington, for instance, did all his early training on British mountains and still has a high regard for the dark brooding Lake District crags and rock faces. Anyway, I watched as the couple set off to disappear among the trees hugging the path just feet from the precipitous drop down to the valley floor.

'Mmm,' was all Tommy would say, nodding into his water bottle as we were eventually alone again with our spectacular view. 'Oh, well, chop, chop.'

I didn't really feel like moving and for once Tommy seemed to have more energy than me. He quickly strapped on his rucksack and moved off, leaving me still relaxed and lethargic. But the sweat on the back of my shirt had gone cold and uncomfortable so I struggled into my rucksack and followed my pal up the path. We must have walked for three-quarters of an hour, pausing to take photographs at the scenic bits, when nearby lightning flashed, followed by a loud clap of thunder followed by more lightening and then some rain came, cooling us. Someone had flicked that weather switch again changing things with a suddenness that happens sometimes in mountain areas.

'This is more like home,' said Tommy, as we paused to get into our waterproofs. Tommy had a new set of waterproofs and this was the first time he'd used them. He donned the matching trousers and top and asked me: 'Do I look the part?'

I told him he was a namby pamby posing bastard as we headed into the wind and rain. Then the wind got stronger on the edge that would have been totally exposed but for the trees, and the branches waved about like demented arms and spiny fingers. It got so bad that at one point we had to hold on to a tree to stop us being blown off the ridge and heavy rain pelted our faces.

'Just like home,' confirmed Tommy, hiding under his hood.

On a particular vertiginous part, where exposed tree roots seemed to be all that was holding the ridge top together, the couple who had passed us earlier were hanging on to sturdy branches for support, holding their faces away from the wind and rain. The woman was shaking and said something about it all being too dangerous and that they wanted to know where the quick path down was.

'This is fun,' said Tommy allowing the pair to get past us. 'I'd go back the way you came,' he added as lightning lit up the darkening sky and the rain increased. It was only five minutes later that the wind became ferocious and we knew that our time on the Niederkaiser ridge had come to an end. Reluctantly we turned back to find a path which meandered steeply downwards through trees. A sign said the Metzgeralm hut and pointed downwards. We took the path down, joining a wider path a few minutes later, but we had to get into some woods to avoid the rain. I have never seen the like of before. The whole air was a sheet of water, torrents turned the path into a river.

'Bit worse than home,' admitted Tommy from somewhere deep under the breathable material of his hood. Then lightning lit up everywhere which was a cue to get away from the trees, so we moved out on to the river that had once been a path, and made our way down towards the Metzgeralm hut and on reaching the hut carried on to a road which eventually took us to Kirchdorf, and only then did it stop raining. Standing at the bus stop on the main road waiting for the bus to Kitzbuhel, we looked much worse than drowned rats, and felt it.

The next day, Thursday, with most of our gear in the hotel drying room, we took a gentle stroll to the Schwarzsee (The Black Lake) which is probably two or three kilometres from Kitzbuhel, a pleasant walk which we took our time on. We had a beer at a restaurant overlooking the lake, then walked back and had a long afternoon sleep before our evening meal.

Friday, our last day of activities, we caught the cable car up to the top of the Hahnenkamm again and joined in the mass route march for a few circuits, had a lazy day, took photographs of lots of mist, then came back down again. (I have amassed an amazing collection of mist photographs over the years.)

On the Saturday, killing time, we sauntered through a park in Kitzbuhel, then fell asleep on a bench under the hot sun. Upon waking, lethargy took over and we sat there, too relaxed to tell jokes, watching the residents of Kitzbuhel enjoying the park paths. When we eventually did move, Tommy's wood homing antenna guided us to some more local joinery achievements, including another bridge, which he proclaimed to be wonderful.

During our stay we did attempt to get the key to the hut which we had stayed in two years previously, but the man we were directed to, who had the key, told us we had to be members of the Alpine Club to stay in the hut, so again we failed in our attempt to get up the Maukspitze. Anyway, the day we had in mind was the day of the awful weather on the Niederkaiser, which was more or less next door to the Maukspitze, so we wouldn't have climbed it anyway.

On this holiday Tommy did not have any bowel problem, although on that last day up on the Hahkenkamm, he did mention that he had a standard to keep up. Before us, on the path, an enormous cow pat, hard and flat, like a pancake, covered a three feet diameter circle. Tommy suggested that we take it back to the hotel and lay it over the WC, to impress the staff.